Praise for *Marriage*

"At Focus on the Family, we hear from couples every day who are struggling in their relationships and desperately seeking healing in their marriages. Through personal and pastoral experience—along with a keen understanding of biblical teaching—Chip Ingram casts a vision for marriage as God intends it. Better yet, he shows readers how to achieve the kind of marriage they've always dreamed of."

Jim Daly, president, Focus on the Family

"This is not just another book on marriage. Chip cuts through political correctness to get to the heart of Christlikeness by challenging both men and women to greater sacrifice in their relationship with one another."

Kyle Idleman, author, *not a fan.* and *Don't Give Up*

"If you are looking for a practical, biblically based picture of marriage, you need look no further. Chip Ingram has nailed it. I highly recommend *Marriage That Works*."

Gary D. Chapman, PhD, author, *The 5 Love Languages*

Praise for *Why I Believe*

"Chip Ingram has a way of taking complex and intimidating material and making it accessible and applicable to everyone."

Kyle Idleman, pastor, author of *Grace Is Greater*

"We all need straight answers to the questions we ask about God, faith, and the Bible. Chip Ingram helps us to get our hearts and minds around the most important issues we face and offers authentic and transparent answers."

Jack Graham, pastor of Prestonwood
Baptist Church, Plano, TX

Praise for *The Real God*

"Chip Ingram provides wonderful insight to help you see God's character as presented in Scripture. In these pages, he offers practical biblical help to live out the implications of a refreshed and renewed perspective of God. The principles in this book will inspire, encourage, and empower you to become more like Jesus Christ."

Rick Warren, founding pastor, Saddleback Church

Praise for *Good to Great in God's Eyes*

"The principles that my good friend Chip Ingram outlines in this book will inspire, encourage, and enable any sincere reader to maximize their God-given potential for the glory of God and for the good of others. Read this only if you want your life to matter."

Tony Evans, PhD, senior pastor,
Oak Cliff Bible Fellowship

I CHOOSE PEACE

I CHOOSE PEACE

HOW TO QUIET YOUR HEART
IN AN ANXIOUS WORLD

CHIPINGRAM

BakerBooks
a division of Baker Publishing Group
Grand Rapids, Michigan

© 2021 by Chip Ingram

Published by Baker Books
a division of Baker Publishing Group
PO Box 6287, Grand Rapids, MI 49516-6287
www.bakerbooks.com

Paper edition published 2023
ISBN 978-1-5409-0128-6

Printed in the United States of America

The Library of Congress has cataloged the original edition as follows:
Names: Ingram, Chip, 1954– author.
Title: I choose peace : how to quiet your heart in an anxious world / Chip Ingram.
Description: Grand Rapids, Michigan : Baker Books, a division of Baker Publishing Group, [2021] | Includes bibliographical references.
Identifiers: LCCN 2020042357 | ISBN 9780801093821 (cloth) | ISBN 9781540901286 (paperback)
Subjects: LCSH: Peace—Religious aspects—Christianity. | Anxiety—Religious aspects—Christianity. | Stress management—Religious Aspects—Christianity. | Bible. Philippians, IV—Criticism, interpretation, etc.
Classification: LCC BV4908.5 .I54 2021 | DDC 248.8/6—dc23
LC record available at https://lccn.loc.gov/2020042357

Baker Publishing Group publications use paper produced from sustainable forestry practices and post-consumer waste whenever possible.

23 24 25 26 27 28 29   7 6 5 4 3 2 1

To the Venture Church family—
elders who became fast friends
and modeled these truths,
staff who practiced them with me,
and a congregation who loved and supported
Theresa and me for nearly a decade.
May the *shalom* of God be in you
and with you all the days of your precious lives.

CONTENTS

Introduction   11

1. Choose Peace in Relational Conflict   15

2. Choose Peace in Anxious Moments   43

3. Choose Peace in a Broken World   67

4. Choose Peace in Difficult Circumstances   97

5. Choose Peace in a Materialistic Culture   125

6. Choose Peace in Tests of Faith   151

Conclusion   181
I Choose Peace Teaching Series Notes   183
Notes   199
References   201

INTRODUCTION

Jesus and His disciples were crossing the Sea of Galilee in a small fishing boat one day when a violent storm swept over the water. Waves crashed over the side of the boat, and the disciples were terrified. They cried out to Jesus for help, but somehow, some way, He was still asleep in the stern. They were overwhelmed with fear for their lives; He was taking a nap. And when they woke Him up and accusingly asked, "Don't you care if we drown?" (Mark 4:38), He didn't thank them for alerting Him to the problem. He simply calmed the storm and asked why they were so faithless and afraid. In circumstances that would make most people panic, Jesus had astonishing, supernatural peace.

If you are a believer and follower of Jesus, you have peace too. Maybe that's news to you. Perhaps you've been struggling and straining to find peace in the midst of tumultuous circumstances and personal crises. Maybe, after discovering that being a Christian doesn't pluck anyone out of all life's problems, you've wondered where that elusive peace is. You know it's a promise in Scripture. You just don't know why you aren't experiencing it. And you might argue with someone who tells you that you already have it.

But I'm telling you anyway. You already have it. Jesus actually gave *His* peace to all His followers the night before His crucifixion. "Peace I leave with you; my peace I give you. I do not give to you as the world gives. Do not let your hearts be troubled and do not be afraid" (John 14:27). So you don't have the kind of peace the world tries to give. You have the peace that Jesus gives—the same peace He had that day in the back of the boat while a storm raged around Him.

So why don't all Christians experience this supernatural peace? Because we must willfully, purposefully choose to walk in the peace He gave us. It isn't automatic. Even though we already have it, we tend to pursue peace on the world's terms. The world offers it to us if and when we are successful, accomplished, pretty, rich, famous, or secure. It holds out an ideal that most people can never attain, and those who do attain that find out it isn't all it's cracked up to be. It promises peace but can't deliver. And in the process, it robs us of the peace we've already been given.

This book will help you overcome the various challenges and lies that rob us of Jesus's peace. We will discover the biblical truths and principles that allow us to experience deep, lasting peace in the midst of relational conflict, anxious moments, the brokenness of this world, difficult circumstances, a materialistic culture, tests of faith, and all the uncertain times we experience in the chaos of life. We will look at the theological basis for experiencing supernatural peace, but the focus is not on theory. It's on actually experiencing it. By the end of the book, you will have numerous practical steps you can take to experience the fullness of the peace Jesus has promised.

This book is not written in a vacuum, an ivory tower, or a pulpit. It comes from decades of experience, much of it hard earned, and observations about how God works. Many of its illustrations come from the hardest times of my life. It was written during a pandemic that threatened the global economy and changed the way we live. And all the adversity, challenges, and crisis situations of life do nothing to change the truths and practices we find in God's Word. In fact, they confirm them. These principles of peace apply in the best and worst of times because they aren't dependent on the times. They are rooted in the nature and character of God Himself.

That means we can have the kind of peace that is available twenty-four hours a day, seven days a week, 365 days a year. It is never beyond our reach if we know how to reach it and take the steps God has given us to experience it. That's my prayer for you in the pages that follow—that you will anchor yourself far deeper than the chaotic circumstances and values of this world and live high above them. And that every day for the rest of your life, your heart, mind, and soul will be filled with the peace that passes all human understanding.

CHAPTER 1

Choose Peace in Relational Conflict

I didn't grow up following Jesus. I went to church, but I never encountered God there and met a lot of people who talked one way and lived another. I didn't know if God existed and really didn't care. I didn't think I needed Him.

Life has a way of pointing out your needs over time, and I had plenty of them. And God has a way of bringing people into your life who can show you what He is like and how He meets those needs. Right after I graduated from high school, I met some people whose lives were radically different from mine. They shared God's love with me and invited me into a personal relationship with Him. They told me Jesus died in my place to break down all the walls between me and God so I could have peace with Him. It was all very new, and I was very skeptical, but I turned from my self-will and sin and asked Jesus to come into my life.

As a new believer, I was given a Bible that was written in easy-to-understand language. No one told me I had to read it, but I couldn't put it down. I even hid it under my pillow; I didn't want my parents to think I'd become a Jesus Freak. But there were some things I couldn't hide. I changed. My insecurities had driven me to be a type A overachiever who just had to date the right girl, get the right scholarship, and accomplish whatever would make me a "somebody." But when my new relationship with God made me a somebody, there was nobody left to impress. He had taken up residence inside me. I had peace.

My father was an alcoholic and a retired Marine (not an ex-Marine, as I was once bluntly corrected). When I came home from college after my first year, he asked what was going on with me.

"What do you mean?" I asked.

"You're different," he said. "Really different."

"What's different about me?"

"There's peace in your life. How'd you get it?"

I was hardly a theologian at the time. It was all very new. So I gave him the best answer I could. "I have no idea. All I can tell you is I have a personal relationship with God and have been reading the New Testament."

"Where do you get one of those?"

I told him, and he started getting up early every morning to read the Bible. Eventually he came to grips with some of his issues and turned his life over to Christ. He began to change too.

Peace is part of the package when we enter into a relationship with God in Christ. It's not always a smooth path—Dad and I both had plenty of ups and downs along the way—but it's ours for the taking. Yet we have to choose it. Peace is a gift and a choice.

> **Peace is a gift and a choice.**

Over the years, I've learned how to determine whether I receive or reject that gift. I've managed to figure out some unfortunate ways to quench God's peace so I don't actually experience it. I know how to worry, stress out, focus on the future, and get into conflict with other people, including my own wife and children, and I've seen the peace dissipate pretty quickly. But I also know by now how to be intentional about it. It's possible to train our hearts and minds to shift our focus and experience the peace we've been given. We really can choose to live in peace and experience God's restoration in our lives.

What Is the Source of Your Peace?

People tend to search for peace from one of three sources. One is *inward*. Advocates of this approach will tell you that you just need to look within. It's already there; you just need to find it. You can do that through meditation, relaxation, centering, and whatever else it takes to find harmony with the cosmos. But it's not "out there" somewhere, and you can't depend on circumstances and other people to give it to you. You have to discover it yourself, somewhere deep inside.

There's some truth to that approach. Circumstances and other people really don't provide peace, and there is some value in going deep within. But what source are you going to find there? Meditation and relaxation are means in a process, not sources. The search within would have to lead to something reliable and true.

Another source people commonly appeal to is *outward*. We are told to achieve, to conquer our fears, to control our emotions and our environment, to perform in ways that lead to lasting peace. It's out there, and we are to discover it by accomplishing something that brings us peace—getting into a good school and making good grades, finding the right person to be with, finding a meaningful and profitable career track, having a nice home and driving a nice car, creating a secure income. The idea is that if we achieve, conquer, and perform, our desires and circumstances will align, and we'll have the peace we're looking for.

The problem with this approach is that the peace that is out there is always just out of reach. There's never enough achievement and success to make life truly peaceful. There's always a situation or two that need to be fixed. There's never quite enough money to completely satisfy us. American oil tycoon J. Paul Getty was the richest person in the world, at one point bringing in $20 million a day, and he was consumed with keeping it going and getting more. He was divorced five times and alienated from his children, often prioritizing money over their health and welfare. Near the end of his life, he said he would gladly give his millions away for just one lasting marital success. He had spent his life accumulating more and more and still had no peace. No matter how much he tried to buy it, it just wasn't "out there."

Eastern traditions tend to emphasize the inward source of peace, while Western traditions have gravitated toward the outward source. And some of these approaches are not inherently wrong in themselves. There's nothing wrong with breathing deeply, relaxing, and centering, on one hand, or earning money, making good grades, and searching for the right relationships on the other. Those can be great skills to have. But they are methods and endeavors that work much better as by-products or outcomes of peace, not the source of it. They can't ground us in reality, and they aren't dependable.

The dependable approach, the one that grounds us in truth, is *upward*. Peace is a person, not a condition (Ephesians 2:14). Jesus said He doesn't give the kind of peace the world gives. He gives His own peace (John 14:27). We trust in Him, depend on Him, and abide in Him. We cultivate faith, love, and obedience to His ways, and He gives His peace to us. We don't discover it within or reach for it outside of ourselves. We receive it by faith.

Peace is a person, not a condition.

When I turned from my sin and invited Christ to forgive me and come into my life, He took up residence in me and sealed me with His Spirit. I didn't know such monumental events happened at the time, but I can look back and see that they did. The Holy Spirit lives inside of those who believe, and through Him we experience God's sovereignty over a chaotic world, the goodness of His nature, and the peace and calm of knowing Him. In fact, peace is one of the fruits of the Spirit (Galatians 5:22). Regardless of whether circumstances go up or down, relationships are good or bad, or the stock market rises or falls, we can have a supernatural peace that transcends human understanding (Philippians 4:7). He will keep us in perfect peace as our minds are stayed on Him (Isaiah 26:3).

God's Peace: *Shalom*

Dictionary definitions of *peace* often describe it as the absence of something—the absence of disturbance and hostility, of internal and external strife, of conflict between people or nations. In other words, it's the calm between the storms, those times of getting along or being at rest that are so often disrupted by crises and turmoil. In fact, many people have a hard time describing peace without focusing on what it is not. But God's definition of peace is different. It's something we can choose, embrace, and enjoy. We don't run away from turmoil to find it. We enter into it. Rather than the absence of some conflict or stress, it's the presence of something God gives.

The Hebrew word for this peace is *shalom*. It's a familiar term for many, and *peace* is the best one-word translation we have for it. But the English word *peace* doesn't nearly capture the meaning of the Hebrew expression. *Shalom* is much bigger. It's a rich, full concept that covers every area of our lives.

There are four aspects of the biblical use of *shalom*: (1) complete wholeness and health; (2) harmony in relationships; (3) success and progress in our purpose; and (4) victory over enemies. So in contrast to the world's peace, God's peace includes our mind, body, and emotions. It covers our marriages and children, relationships with neighbors and coworkers, and fellowship with other members of the body of Christ. Our alignment with God, His purpose for our lives, and the ability to live in His will are all involved—no matter how many ups and downs we go through in following Him and walking out His plans. And this *shalom* encompasses confidence that He is protecting us, providing for us, helping us overcome difficult problems and adversaries, and giving us victories in life's challenges.

We will face those challenges, sometimes long-lasting ones, in every one of these aspects of *shalom*. Some people spend nearly their whole lives wondering if they are in the right job or the right place or if they are with the right person. Many of us live with the dreaded fear of missing out, that FOMO that keeps us thinking of alternatives almost constantly. At some point we will have conflict with somebody, face challenges that seem insurmountable, struggle with physical and emotional issues, and search for God's will for our lives. But we can trust that God will lead us toward *shalom* in every area of our lives as His stated purpose for each of us. He wants us to have peace in all its fullness.

Jesus is the Prince of Peace (Isaiah 9:6), literally the Prince of *Shalom*. The night before His crucifixion, He told His followers that He was giving them His *shalom*. "Peace I leave with you; my peace I give you. I do not give to you as the world gives. Do not let your hearts be troubled and do not be afraid" (John 14:27). That's more than a promise of a calm demeanor in a moment of crisis. *Shalom* is a comprehensive expression of God's will for us in every situation we face.

> ### *Shalom* is a comprehensive expression of God's will for us in every situation we face.

"Do not let your hearts be troubled and do not be afraid." What a great line for us—an assurance of the peace of God in any area where we feel unsettled. When you're watching the news and feel threatened by a rapidly spreading disease or an economic downturn; when you're worried about your future, whether you will ever find the right job, get married, have children, and have good, satisfying relationships through it all; when you're looking around you and seeing all the things people are dealing with in this world, you need that kind of assurance. The good news is that God gives it to us.

That doesn't mean everything will always work out just the way we want it to. It does mean, however, that we can live our entire lives as followers of Christ with supernatural peace. Some people go through their whole lives with that kind of peace available to them and never choose it. They are robbed of something that was theirs for the taking. The purpose of this book—and God's purpose for our lives—is to give us the understanding and the tools to avoid that tragedy.

In the first five chapters, we're going to look at five things that rob us of our peace. Paul covers them in Philippians 4, and the first is conflict in a relationship. Some of us get along with nearly everybody, while others have a hard time getting along with anybody. But all of us have someone in our lives with whom we would like to have a better relationship. If you had to come up with a person who is at odds with you (or you with them), whether in your family or somewhere else in your social network, whether now or buried in the distant past, who would it be? Maybe you can think of several, but my guess is one person came to mind first. Who is that?

Whoever that is—an old friend, an in-law, an ex-spouse, a contentious coworker—you can't experience your God-given *shalom* if you push it down and cover it up, or if you always think the problem is all the other person's fault and none of your own. Whatever lack of relationship health you don't deal with, whatever poison or bitterness eats away at you will affect you somehow. It may color your healthy relationships in negative ways, unsettle your emotions, or manifest in physical issues like indigestion and migraines. Whatever the case, you need to be at peace in your relationships, at least as far as it depends on you. Full reconciliation may not always be possible, but it is possible to know you've done everything you can do and be content with that. In the following pages, we are going to walk through a biblical process for getting peace when you have relational conflict.

Dealing with Relational Conflict

● *The Context*

When Paul wrote Philippians, he was in confinement in Rome—probably under house arrest awaiting a trial for crimes he didn't commit. He deeply loved the church at Philippi, where he had also been in prison, though just for one very dramatic night. God had done amazing things in this church, and Paul thought of it fondly. It was one of the bright spots of his ministry.

But there were a few problems in Philippi, and when we read between the lines of his letter, we can see that some people may have been drifting away from God and forgetting the importance and the power of the gospel in their lives. There was also apparently some relational conflict, some sort of personality clash or competitive spirit between some of the members. So Paul wrote to remind them of his love, to encourage them to stand firm, to urge them to plant their feet in the kingdom of heaven where their true citizenship was, and to give them hope in the midst of the mess of this world.

He ends chapter 3 with these reminders and a call to live out their new, heavenly life on earth. And in that context, he turns his attention to the two people who need to remember that heavenly citizenship in the midst of their relationship. These two women might have expected a stern rebuke, a command to get with the program and behave, but that's not the heart behind Paul's words. He was encouraging them to remember who they were, who God is, and how their hope applies to life in this world. Listen to his tender but strong words to each of them.

"Therefore, my brothers and sisters, you whom I love and long for, my joy and crown, stand firm in the Lord in this way, dear friends!" (Philippians 4:1). Those are not the words of an angry leader. They are the words of an encouraging friend. These people are his *joy* and his *crown* whom he *loves* and *longs for*. He is telling them that when they don't live in the peace God provides, it breaks his heart. He wants them to stand firm in the hope they have been given.

● The Plea

Then Paul issues a direct plea for unity and request for counsel:

> I plead with Euodia and I plead with Syntyche to be of the same mind in the Lord. Yes, and I ask you, my true companion, help these women since they have contended at my side in the cause of the gospel, along with Clement and the rest of my co-workers, whose names are in the book of life. (Philippians 4:2–3)

These are two good women. Paul is not looking for fault here. No one is "the bad guy." From the context, we can tell that this is not a moral or a doctrinal issue. Perhaps they disagree about how the church ought to function, or maybe their personalities just rub each other the wrong way. We don't know. But we do know that Paul sees them as strong and faithful members of this church who have been greatly used by God. They have contended with him, "at [his] side" as his right and left hands, in the growing of this church. They have been instrumental in the strength of this church through its beginnings and its opposition and challenges. Their names are written in the Book of Life. For whatever reason, they aren't getting along now. And, as in any family or small group, conflict between two people affects the others.

So Paul pleads with these women to agree, literally to have the same mind. He also asks a "true companion" to help them—to intervene in the situation and give them counsel. Sometimes two people can't resolve their own differences. They need help. There's nothing wrong with that. It's how the body of Christ works to bring unity and peace.

The phrase "true companion," or "loyal yokefellow" in some translations, is the Greek *syzygos*, which describes a strong bond between two parties—in marriage, labor (like two oxen bound together), or with a very close companion. Here it could refer to one of Paul's partners in ministry—an idea that has led to plenty of speculation about this person's identity—or it could be read as a proper name. In any case, the meaning fits very nicely with the point of Paul's plea, which is aimed at getting people to walk together in peace and harmony. The small church, which likely met in someone's home at this point, had a problem. Conflict, resentment, competitiveness, and whatever other dynamics that were involved were affecting the whole group. Paul recognized someone there who probably had the gift of exhortation and wise counsel, and he wanted that person to sit down with these women and help.

The Commands

Next Paul gives two commands. The first deals with this church's relational focus. It's easy in the midst of a conflict to focus on the problem, specifically on the other person's faults, motives, offenses, and attitudes. We replay events and conversations in our minds, fixate on whatever part of the relationship is bad (even if most of it is good), and begin to demonize the other person. We harden our hearts, nurse our wounds, and cultivate our anger. And anger that simmers long enough begins to boil over. Our focus makes the problem worse. So Paul tells them to change their focus.

"Rejoice in the Lord always. I will say it again: Rejoice!" (Philippians 4:4). We may read these words as a nice encouragement, but in context, it's a command. Paul is telling them to get their eyes off horizontal relationships among human beings and put them on their vertical relationship with God. This command is not just for the two women at odds with each other; it's for the whole church. He doesn't want them to take sides, to try to figure out who's right and wrong or how this power struggle is going to play out. That's our tendency, isn't it? We develop cliques and factions, and small conflicts turn into big ones. We find people who agree with us, and the stakes get higher. If we want to have peace, we have to shift our focus from people to God.

> **If we want to have peace, we have to shift our focus from people to God.**

Try going to a coffee shop sometime and listen to everybody's conversations. Pretend like you're doing something on your phone or your laptop but tune in to what's going on around you. "I don't know what he's thinking, but . . ." "He plays golf three times a week and expects me to take care of the kids!" "I can't believe my roommate; I don't know how much longer I can do this." "My supervisor must be on drugs." What are these people doing? Gathering people to their cause, building up their side, stirring up animosity against someone else. It's like pouring gasoline on a fire. You can't imagine that these conversations are actually making anything better.

What would make things better is a change in focus. Turning our attention to God, rejoicing in all that He has done, celebrating the life and promises He has given us—that radical shift in attitude quenches a lot of fires. Some things are much more important than making sure we are happy in a situation and getting the respect we think we deserve. Recognizing the bigger issues makes our other issues look a lot smaller.

Recognizing the bigger issues makes our other issues look a lot smaller.

Then Paul gives a second command: "Let your gentleness be evident to all. The Lord is near" (Philippians 4:5). These believers have a personal responsibility to each other. Instead of putting the blame on the other person, they are to have enough humility to take the lead in resolving the problem. Why? Because the Lord is near.

The Lord's nearness could be taken in two ways: either that He is close by and available, watching us in our conflicts and offering solutions for them; or that He is coming back soon, which is consistent with Paul's words at the end of chapter 3. Whether the focus of this passage is Jesus's availability or our accountability in light of His return, the application is the same. Life is short. We will all face Him soon enough. It's important to live with that perspective.

That implies living with a sense of *gentleness*. No single English word translates this Greek concept well, but it includes tolerance, forbearance, geniality, generosity, kindness, and humility. One commentator calls it "sweet reasonableness."[1] Paul is essentially telling them to be willing not to get their way in the relationship for the sake of the reputation of Christ and His people. In other words, we don't have to be proved right. We don't have to establish the fact that we are only 5 percent at fault. We can go ahead and own 51 percent and get the ball moving because it's more important for things to be right than for us to be right. That takes a lot of humility. And Paul says to make it "evident" to all.

> **It's more important for things to be right than for us to be right.**

Five Ways to Defuse Relational Conflict

Relationships matter to God. We don't just choose peace for our own sakes, although we greatly benefit from doing so. We choose peace because God seeks reconciliation with everyone, and we are being conformed to His image. It's a reflection of His nature. So resolving conflict has a lot to do with following Him well.

Reconciliation isn't easy when we think we know how the other person is going to respond. We often adopt a "why try?" attitude. But we try for the same reasons Paul urged Euodia and Syntyche to resolve their differences and because God says to make every effort. So if your network of relationships is ruptured, especially in a relationship with a family member or other member of the body of Christ, seek peace as diligently as you can. Be very intentional and persistent in following these steps toward restoration.

1. Resolve to stop procrastinating. Make a commitment to address the problem. Whichever relationship first came to mind when we started this chapter, think of a specific step you can take toward reconciliation. Maybe it begins with a conversation, an appointment with a counselor, or even a prayer for God to help you as you walk this out. Whatever moves you in that direction, be decisive about it and commit to it.

Why is it so important to stop procrastinating? Because a lack of peace in your relationships adds stress to your life and affects your physical and emotional health. You may not feel it happening—sometimes the stress is very subtle—but the harmful effects are doing something to you beneath the surface. Many people who wrestle with addictions aren't primarily facing a problem with food, shopping, porn, alcohol, or drugs. They are covering up the pain of a broken relationship and a wounded heart. When you lack peace, you try to calm an unsettled soul with all sorts of short-term remedies that mask the pain but heal nothing. And the fixes that give you artificial peace keep demanding more and more of you. You have to address the problem at its core.

You have to address the problem at its core.

Through Paul's pen, God instructs us to do just that. "Be careful to do what is right in the eyes of everyone. If it is possible, as far as it depends on you, live at peace with everyone" (Romans 12:17–18). *Everyone* means everyone—Christians, non-Christians, family members, coworkers, supervisors, neighbors, everyone. The term for "be careful to do" means "to consider." It's an accounting term, a reckoning, a thoughtful appraisal of the situation. That approach takes us out of all the "he did this" and "she did that" reasonings that go on in our minds. It enables us to see from someone else's perspective and try to understand why they think they are right. Perhaps it helps us recognize that they are gifted in different ways or have a different background that informs their perspective. It puts us in a position to quit being defensive and think objectively. Understanding the situation is the necessary first step toward any kind of resolution, restitution, healing, or forgiveness.

2. Reevaluate your expectations. Some of us got the idea somewhere in our spiritual development that Christians should never argue—that if we are really being spiritual, our relationships will always be harmonious. That means if we have a falling out with someone, that person must be unspiritual, disobedient—maybe even just bad.

In Philippians 4, there isn't a bad person creating problems for the church. We see two women who have contended for the faith and whose names are written in the Book of Life—and, as Paul may be thinking, are going to have to spend an eternity together and might as well start getting along now. But at the moment, even though they are committed Christians and God has worked through each of them, not everything is wonderful between them. That happens. We can't expect that Christians will never make mistakes, offend anyone, or speak thoughtless words. We can't assume Christian relationships are always smooth.

Sometimes we're shocked by what other Christians do—how Christian businesspeople work, how Christian leaders lead, how Christian families get dysfunctional like other families do. Some Christians are "rescuers" who just want everything to get fixed, and others are "warriors" who just want people to recognize how wrong they are and own their stuff. We expect other people to behave in certain ways, and we're shocked or disappointed when they don't. Whatever solution you tend to play out in your imagination—other people coming to grips with their mistakes and confessing how wrong they were, or some great revelation that makes it all a huge misunderstanding—things probably aren't going to happen that way. We'll never find genuine reconciliation or experience genuine peace until we get past those unbiblical and unrealistic expectations.

Conflict is real, and Christians aren't immune to it. Paul could testify to that himself. He and Barnabas had a strong relationship that went back to Paul's earliest days as a believer, when only Barnabas trusted his conversion and helped him out. Years later, they were sent out together on a missionary journey—Paul with his gift of communicating the gospel and Barnabas, the "son of encouragement," planting numerous churches and spreading the gospel far and wide. But when the time came for a second journey, they had "such a sharp disagreement that they parted company" (Acts 15:39). Barnabas wanted to include a young believer named John Mark, who had quit on the first journey and went home, and Paul didn't want to go through that again. So Paul took Silas because he felt like he could trust him, Barnabas took John Mark probably because he thought it would be good for him, and they went their separate ways.

We don't know all the details of that story, but we know that for an encouraging, generous personality like Barnabas to part company with a high-powered, driven personality like Paul—after they had worked so closely, been so fruitful, and ministered to each other in times of great need—it had to be an extremely contentious situation. This wasn't a case of two men weighing the pros and cons and deciding that perhaps it would be in their mutual interests to split this into two trips rather than one. Apparently, they blew up at each other. They each had certain expectations of the other that weren't met.

People have different styles, philosophies, and personalities. Sometimes they disagree, not over some crucial doctrinal or moral issue but simply over the way to do things. There's nothing wrong with agreeing to go separate ways. But it isn't right or healthy for the relationship to end in anger, resentment, bitterness, and brokenness.

3. Get competent outside help. Sometimes God will put it on your heart to seek restoration in a relationship, yet everything you try seems to make it worse. This can be especially painful in a close, long-term relationship with a spouse or other family member, but it's also frustrating with friends, coworkers, small-group members, a business relationship, or anywhere else you experience ongoing friction. In any relationship, there's no shame in asking for help.

In most relationships, that can be as simple as having a trusted friend to mediate or offer counsel. In the really big relationships like marriage and family, it may mean getting professional help. That's really difficult for many people, especially men. Some of us avoid the touchy-feely stuff or think counseling is for people with "real problems," which of course is never us. Usually those expressions are just another way of saying we feel really threatened in that area and don't want to look too closely at our own lives. We run from the tools that could help us the most because they might be painful to use.

In any relationship, there's no shame in asking for help.

That's where I was early in my marriage. I was in seminary, learning to preach the Word of God to others, and I couldn't even get along with my own wife. We didn't have much income, and professional help can be expensive, even at a student rate. But the bigger issue for me was a stubborn, arrogant pride. It was extremely difficult for me to admit that Theresa and I might need some help. I struggled to overcome my inward resistance and swallow my pride, finally realizing it was the only way to improve my marriage.

We had another little bump five years later, and this time it wasn't as big a deal. By this point, I'd learned that humility is the channel grace flows through. We had been talking for hours and realized we weren't making any progress, so we decided to go talk with someone we trusted who could look at it objectively from a biblical point of view. It was amazing, and it helped us find some resolution.

When you get help from someone objective—not your friend or the other person's friend, but someone who will treat you equally—you'll probably hear some things you don't want to hear. You'll learn something about yourself. Both of you will walk away having decided not to demand that the other person change for the relationship to be what it needs to be. You can't control the other person, but you can be responsible for yourself. And if you choose to work on your own issues, whether the other person responds or not, you're well on the way to improving your relationship and ultimately to restoration.

> **Humility is the channel grace flows through.**

4. Refuse to allow one relationship to ruin your life. Human beings have lots of ways to get offended, and some of them are legitimate. It happens in churches a lot. You lead a Bible study but have to be away for a week, and the next year the leadership asks the person who filled in for you to lead the study this time. Or someone moves the flowers you arranged for a funeral, puts you in a different spot on a ministry team, or disrupts the routine you've gotten used to over the last two decades. Offenses turn into animosities, and animosities hold us captive. We have to get free from them.

A young woman came up to me in tears after a service years ago and talked about how her dad left when she was fourteen. Understandably, this was a traumatic experience for her, the kind that can leave deep wounds for a long time. She'd had no relationship with him since that time, and she was captive to her pain. Her wounds were completely legitimate, but I had to ask her if she was going to give him that kind of power. The broken relationship clearly wasn't her fault, but it had still left her hurting. Could she forgive him and leave that pain in the past? It's a hard thing to do, but it's the only way to be free.

Offenses turn into animosities, and animosities hold us captive.

Many people have a relationship like that—with an ex-spouse, an alienated child, a friend or business partner who betrayed us. We'll talk about how to start a conversation in those situations without letting it blow up in your face, but there's something else that has to come first. You have to make a decision not to let that one relationship ruin your life. The other person may not respond well when you take a step toward reconciliation, but having done all you can to fix things, you can step back and be at peace. "If it is possible, as far as it depends on you, live at peace with everyone" (Romans 12:18). Sadly, it's not always possible. But once we've done all we can, we can then "let it go" and be at peace.

Years ago I went through one of the hardest times of my life. I felt like I'd been betrayed. I'm sure my perspective was only partly true, but I was so angry I couldn't sleep. My stomach would churn if I didn't distract myself with music in the car. I kept reliving scenes with certain people and the things they had said and done. It was eating away at me.

One day a friend who was helping me through this told me to "get vertical." That wasn't news to me, but I needed the reminder. I'd been a pastor for years and knew what to do, but it felt impossible to do it. It was good to be pushed in that direction.

Then this friend asked if I would do him a favor.

"Sure," I said.

"I can see that you've gotten some raw deals here. But I want you to meet me here next week at this time, okay?"

"Yeah, okay."

"And I want you to pray for seven days. I want you to list all the mistakes throughout this whole situation as God reveals them to you. In addition, think of all the specific ways you sinned against the people you can't stop thinking about."

This was my friend, a godly guy I trusted, but he didn't seem very friendly right then. But I did what he said, and I remember coming back and sitting in the same place, leaning forward with tears in my eyes, and telling him how I had pushed all those people's buttons. I listed all my leadership mistakes. And even though it was hard to confess some things as sin, I wrote down what God showed me and gave him the list.

You have to make a decision not to let that one relationship ruin your life.

It's amazing how often we demand justice in our relationships with other people but expect mercy in our relationship with God. That was a turning point in my life because I realized I couldn't ask God to give me mercy for all the things I had done and justice for all the things that had been done to me. And in that process, I was able to let it all go. Nothing got fixed, and no circumstances changed. The people I was angry with may have never seen things any differently than they did before. But I could let it go and be at peace.

You can refuse to let a broken relationship ruin your life.

That's how it may be for you. The situation may not be fixed, the relationship may not be restored, you may never shake hands or hug each other again, and there may be no bow to tie up the package neatly. But you can agree to disagree, you can forgive, and you can move forward. You can refuse to let a broken relationship ruin your life.

5. Remember that a right response is more important than being right. I recently had an intense conversation with a young man and realized I'd just poured cold water on his confidence. I regretted it immediately. I went home and went to bed, and that night I found myself in one of those situations when God wakes you up and suddenly makes things clear. *What am I going to do?* I wondered. Human nature always wants to defend itself, of course, so I started to rehearse all the reasons and justifications for saying what I said: *He needs to grow up. Learning to lead means telling people hard things. He'll get over it. I'm older and wiser . . .* And God said, "I'll take care of all that. What about your part?" I knew I had to deal with some things.

Own your part and then some. If you're like me at all, you're guiltier and more messed up than you think. Your perspective doesn't quite go as far as it should toward objectivity.

If you think a conflict is 25 percent your fault, just assume it's probably 50 or 60 percent. That's how it works with me, and I'm pretty sure I'm not alone.

I realized the only thing I could do to make things right was to tell him I was sorry. I typed up an email apologizing for saying certain things, being defensive and too intense, and so on. I just needed to repent. I saw the same guy a couple of days later, and he was so supportive and loving. "I got your email," he said. "You're forgiven." And I was at peace again.

Own your part and then some.

That's normal. This is how it should be. If you want to accomplish something with your life, have a good marriage, have a great relationship with your kids, and work with other people to do something important, there are going to be sparks at certain points along the way. Count on it. And count on being uncomfortable with it. That's just the way it is. But you can deal with it in ways that don't throw gasoline on the fire. You can speak the truth and cover it in love. You can resolve conflict and restore relationships. You can choose peace.

These five steps offer a biblical template for the kind of reconciliation that reflects God's love and prioritizes His peace in our lives. You can find a lot of other relationship advice out there, some of it helpful and some of it not, but one resource I've found very useful for myself and others I've counseled is a book called *Crucial Conversations*.[2] Several people recommended it to me, and it's a great tool for saying hard things in a loving, nonthreatening way. The important thing is to make a commitment to choose peace in your relationships and take initiative to get there. Let love be your motivation, and let God be your guide.

One of the most important things you can do as a next step is to ask Jesus to lead you. Take a few minutes to reflect on the state of your relational health. Pray that He would show you what He wants you to do. Ask Him to put His finger on anything that needs your attention, any broken or damaged relationship that would benefit from your steps toward reconciliation and restoration. And trust Him to walk with you every step of the way.

Let love be your motivation, and let God be your guide.

QUESTIONS FOR DISCUSSION AND REFLECTION

1. On a scale of 1–10, how would you rank the level of stress and concern you are currently experiencing from any problem relationship?

2. Why does relational conflict rob us of peace? What price are you paying to allow this to continue?

3. What specific steps does Paul give to help us resolve relational conflict? Which ones would be most challenging for you? Why?

4. Is there a relationship in your life that calls for you to follow this pattern? When and how will you follow God's plan for peace (as far as it depends on you)?

5. Who could help you turn your good intention into action this week?

CHAPTER 2

Choose Peace
in Anxious Moments

oratio Spafford was an attorney in Chicago when the Great Chicago Fire destroyed much of the city in 1871. He lost most of his investments in that fire, and it took a while to get on his feet again. He thought it would be good to get away for a vacation, and his friend D. L. Moody was planning to preach in England, so he arranged to take his wife and four daughters to Europe.

Not long before the trip, he had to deal with some zoning issues with one of his properties, so he sent his wife and daughters ahead and promised to join them soon. But he received a distressing telegram from his wife during their journey: "Saved alone." Their ship had collided with an-other, and all his daughters died in the shipwreck.

On his way to meet his wife in England, the captain of Spaf-ford's ship pointed out the place where the ships had col-lided and his daughters had died. As Spafford looked out over the ocean and saw the billowing waves, his pain still fresh from his tragic losses, he was moved to write a hymn. "When peace like a river attendeth my way, when sorrows like sea billows roll," it began. It is still widely sung in churches today. "It Is Well with My Soul" is a touching and profound testimony of the peace we can experience even in our most distressing moments.

It's hard to imagine a song of such tremendous peace being written in the face of such heart-wrenching circumstances. Yet that's exactly the kind of peace Jesus promised the night before His crucifixion, knowing His followers were going to be thrown into anxious, tumultuous, painfully trying times the next day. "I have told you these things, so that in me you may have peace," He told them. "Take heart! I have overcome the world" (John 16:33). Trials will come, but they can't destroy us. We can overcome them and have peace in the process.

Trials will come, but they can't destroy us.

Spafford is just one person among mil-lions who have experienced God's peace that passes human understanding. He may have had more anxious and tragic moments than most of us do, but we all have them. We lose loved ones, face uncertain futures, deal with alarming or devastating news, and encounter frustrating and futile experiences. We go through sudden twists and turns in our personal lives and in world events—a pandemic that disrupts our financial, work, and social lives; a volatile economy; wars and natural disasters; the death of a loved one; or any number of other tragic circumstances. Many people go through them all with high stress, raw nerves, and deep-seated anxieties. But we don't have to. Like Horatio Spafford, we can choose peace even in the midst of our most difficult times.

Understanding Our Anxiety

What is anxiety? The books define it as uneasiness, apprehension, dread, concern, tension, restlessness, and worry, and tell us that people get anxious when facing misfortune, danger, or doom. But that doesn't really explain very much, does it? That describes where what many of us experience throughout each week.

The New Testament word for *anxiety* means to "care for" or "take thought." Sometimes it's positive, but usually it refers to an inability to get our minds off of something, perhaps even an obsession. In German, it comes from the word for choking or strangling, which feels very appropriate for us at times. At its heart, the New Testament word suggests pulling us in two different directions and causing enormous stress on our emotions.

Our anxiety can come from several causes. The most common is probably a fear of the future. We are well aware of all the bad things that can and do happen: health problems, financial crises, abandonment, divorce, rejection, problems with our kids, pandemics, terrorist attacks, failures in any area of life, and a multitude of other possibilities both private and public. We hope for the best, but we often worry about the worst. Anxiety becomes a part of our lives.

Anxiety can also be caused by conflict in the present—stresses in marriage, with kids, at work, with neighbors, with in-laws, and so on. And some wrestle with anxiety about the past—regrets that pop up at any given moment, those things we wish had never happened and hope no one ever finds out about. Those of us who came to Christ after years of living without Him can recall plenty of mistakes we made beforehand, but those aside, we are all aware that mistakes don't end at conversion. There are things we can't change about our past, and when memories of them surface—along with a heavy sigh and a softly muttered "I blew it"—they produce anxiety. It can be overwhelming. A drink or a pill can't fix it. Anxiety can ruin our lives.

Anxiety can ruin our lives.

Anxiety has horrible effects. A textbook on psychological disorders identifies numerous spiritual, mental, and emotional by-products of anxious thoughts. It can make people hyperalert, irritable, fidgety, and overdependent. It can cause insomnia, fainting, excessive perspiration, muscle tension, headaches (including migraines), quivering voices, hyperventilation, abdominal pain, nausea, diarrhea, and high blood pressure.[1] That's a pretty scary list, and it makes me want to get rid of anxiety as quickly as I can.

How to Overcome Anxiety

How do you deal with your anxiety when you wake up in the middle of the night and can't get your fears about the future out of your mind long enough to go back to sleep? What do you do when your stomach keeps churning and your neck is perpetually tight because you can't handle the stress? It's one thing to identify anxiety, another to figure out what to do with it. We have to be able to change our thought patterns.

You do not have to live with anxiety. It is possible to have complete peace in the midst of difficult, uncertain, troubling times. We know this is true because Jesus promised that we could. And His Word gives us the tools to do it.

> **We have to be able to change our thought patterns.**

Imagine a kid coming home from school Friday afternoon and pitching his bookbag into the corner of his room. "No homework! It's the weekend!" He isn't thinking about the homework that will be coming in the future or the assignments from earlier in the week. He has taken his load off and set his mind free, at least for the next few days.

That's the picture Peter gives us. "Cast all your anxiety on him because he cares for you" (1 Peter 5:7). It's like taking off a heavy burden and throwing it into the arms of someone who can handle it easily. Those problems, struggles, and fears are no longer yours. You're free from the responsibility. You entrust them to the hands of someone else—a personal God who is in control, who has no lack of wisdom, who is all-powerful, and who sees the future perfectly. And He is not begrudging about taking care of you. You are the object of His affection. You can release everything to Him and know He is always going to handle it with your best interests in mind.

So the key to overcoming anxiety is releasing the things that cause it—not the situations themselves, of course, but the weight of them, the fears and stresses and regrets that contribute to an anxious life. We give our past, present, and future to the God who sees and redeems all of it and who works everything together for the good of those who love Him (Romans 8:28). We will never encounter a single moment in which the grace for dealing with that moment is lacking. We can trust God to be with us and carry us through all of life. He knows how to handle everything.

> **We will never encounter a single moment in which the grace for dealing with that moment is lacking.**

Dealing with Your Anxieties

Paul gives us a specific game plan for dealing with anxiety whenever it comes knocking on the door of our mind and heart. He shows us how to cast our cares on the Lord, as Peter instructed, and how to receive peace in their place. Every time anxiety surfaces within us, we can run into the Father's arms and have His peace instead.

> Do not be anxious about anything, but in every situation, by prayer and petition, with thanksgiving, present your

requests to God. And the peace of God, which transcends
all understanding, will guard your hearts and your minds
in Christ Jesus. (Philippians 4:6–7)

If we look at the mechanics of the original text, we notice
some pretty interesting things in the way certain words are
emphasized. The first instruction here is literally, "Nothing
be anxious about." It's a negative command, and it's worded
strongly to emphasize *nothing*. Stop being anxious. Quit
worrying. This is not a small issue. It can eat up your soul,
distort your emotions, undermine your relationships, and
choke the life out of you. Stop it.

God and His inspired writers in Scripture don't give us
commands without providing the power and the tools to
obey them. So Paul continues with a positive command:
"But in everything." He gives us four specific words to do
in "everything"—in every situation and especially in every
anxiety-producing circumstance: *prayer*, *petition*, *thanksgiving*, *requests*.

The New Testament uses four different words for prayer, and
all of them are in this verse. The point? Whenever anxiety
knocks on the door of your heart, let prayer answer it. That's
your primary response.

But this is not just prayer in general. By using this range of
words, Paul gives us some very specific ways to pray that
address those waking hours in the middle of the night, that
churning stomach, those mental projections into an upset-
ting future concerning your health, your job, your kids, your
marriage, or whatever else you tend to worry about. When

your mind starts to go down that well-worn track, these prayers will turn it back in the right direction and quiet those fears.

That's the promise—that when you offer your prayers and petitions with thanksgiving in your heart, making your requests known to God, His peace will enter in and guard your heart and mind. It will shift the focus of your thoughts onto truth.

The word *guard* means that when you pray like this, the Holy Spirit monitors and protects the deepest parts of your thought life and warns you when something is wrong. He acts like the red light on your dashboard that tells you to look under the hood. When you lose your peace, you have turned your focus from Christ to something else, and He becomes an arbitrator or monitor warning you to get back into that place of abiding in Him. He keeps you in peace.

That's an overview of the grammar and mechanics of these verses and the words they use, but we need to go deeper in learning how to apply them because that's where our anxieties live—in the depths of our hearts and minds. Let's go back and look at these instructions a little more closely.

Applying the Commands to Your Life

We've seen that Paul issues both a negative and a positive command. The negative command is not just an encouraging pat on the back that tells us worry is unnecessary. It's actually a command: *stop worrying about anything.* Then the positive command is just as insistent and powerful: *pray about everything.* These are two sides of the same coin, a behavior to stop and a behavior to begin, a way to reverse the current of your thoughts, turning them in the opposite direction of where you have always taken them.

That may feel like forcing a river to flow upstream. That's because many of us have practiced being anxious most of our lives. We learned from our parents; our peers; the media that bombards us every day with the terrible, tragic, fearful news going on in our world; and our culture in general. Almost everyone is well trained in anxiety, and almost everyone has certain ways of coping with it, medically or with distractions that cover it up.

Many of us have practiced being anxious most of our lives.

So we live in a society of escape—through TV, shopping, a glass of wine, prescriptions, work, food, sex, and myriad other ways to mask, cover, distract, and medicate. There is nothing wrong with any of these things in their proper place, of course; entertainment, food and drink, medications, and all the rest are normal and often necessary for daily life. There are healthy ways to engage with them. But they aren't good substitutes for emotional health. They create the illusion of peace for a moment but never actually give us peace. There's a vast difference between relief and restoration. Some of these things give us a sense of control when life feels out of control, and some just change the way we feel for a time—usually a very short time. We address our anxiety in all sorts of ways, and most of them aren't very helpful.

My personal false mechanisms for appeasing my anxiety are sports and work. Somehow watching other people play games makes me feel better for a while. Sometimes I'll immerse myself in some project that occupies my mind and prevents it from going to anxious places. You'll never hear me preach or write about the evils of sports and work because both of those are perfectly normal and good activities. But when they are substitutes for prayer and the peace of God, there's a problem. When we're trying to get our minds off of a gnawing anxiety, we are just relieving a symptom.

We live in a society of escape.

We aren't actually changing anything, and the anxiety almost always comes back later, sometimes much stronger. Distracting our minds and silencing our hearts is not at all the same as letting the peace of Christ rule in our hearts and minds.

The command to pray about everything is a great way to address our anxieties, but it's important to notice that Paul is talking about some very specific kinds of prayer in this passage. There's nothing wrong with a desperate plea to God in an anxious moment—*Oh God, help me, please, help me, God.* You've been there, I'm sure. We all face challenging crises, and a believer's instinct as God's child is to cry out to Him. But I think God wants to teach us how we can pray purposefully and effectively. Otherwise, we pick up those backpacks filled with burdens as soon as the crisis passes and start carrying them again until the next crisis comes. So Paul identifies some specific ways to pray that will enable us to cast our burdens on God and let His peace come in.

How We Pray: Four Very Important Words

Our prayers are characterized by four words in the New Testament, all of them included in Philippians 4:6. If we understand the meaning of these four specific words and put them into practice, anxiety will begin to dissipate from our hearts and minds, and God's peace will begin to rule there.

● *Prayer*

Proseuche is the most common word in the New Testament for prayer. It involves turning our thoughts and feelings upward the moment we feel anxious, shifting our focus to God. It includes pausing, recognizing what's going on, worshiping and adoring God for who He is, and acknowledging that He is greater than our struggles.

I have to admit, I've had more than a few struggles with anxiety over the years. I tend to juggle more balls than I can handle and try to accomplish more than I'm actually capable of doing. Sometimes when I wake up, the first thought in my mind is about the day's to-do list—meetings, projects, events to prepare for, responsibilities with family members, and tons of other things that just have to get done. And then I check my phone or email and see that the Dow has dropped, a problem at work has come up, and something I didn't anticipate needs to be dealt with right away. If you're like me, you know how that kind of start to your day can set you up for disaster. What I've learned to do to combat mornings like this is to begin by spiritually, mentally, and emotionally bringing my life and everything in it to God.

The first thing you need to do every morning is pray—say the Lord's Prayer, recite Psalm 23, or find some other verse or prayer that immediately prioritizes your relationship with God and puts your focus on Him. I've learned that if I don't see life through God's lens, I'm going to be in big trouble. Life will bring challenges that I'm not prepared for. Even the ones I already have are more than I can handle. I have to start out with something that casts current and potential burdens on Him.

Jesus began the model prayer with the words "Our Father." In the midst of the world's craziness and messes, we can acknowledge that the One who is sovereign, who sent His Son to die for our sins, who is all-wise, all-knowing, and all-powerful, is our Father in heaven, our Papa who loves us beyond our wildest imaginations. We can trust Him. He won't lie to us, His intentions toward us are always good, and He's in control of everything.

So I've developed the habit of praying while I'm still lying in bed, slowly going through Psalm 23 or the Lord's Prayer, worshiping my Father who loves me. Then when I get up, I don't check my email. I have my coffee, I let the dog out, and I stand on the patio and look up. Out loud, I say something like this: "Almighty, ever-living Creator, little people like me have stared at the stars in this sky for thousands and thousands of years, and this is only a tiny fraction of the ones You've created—a few among the two hundred billion stars in this little galaxy, with another couple hundred billion galaxies beyond. At this moment, on this day, I am the object of Your affection. I'm going to go in and talk to You and listen to what You want to say to me in Your Word. I don't know what's going to happen or how to pull off anything I need to do, but I'm going into this day with You, the Creator of the world, at my back and Your Holy Spirit at my side."

If you get a clear, high view of God like that every morning, your day is off to a great start. Your God gets really big and your problems get really small very quickly. Our anxieties make problems big and God small, and this kind of prayer returns us to the right perspective. Human nature and anxious thoughts focus in on the problem areas of our lives. If our marriage is 90 percent good, we tend to obsess about the 10 percent that isn't. If work is going really well except for that one supervisor who keeps causing problems, we can't stop thinking about the supervisor. If our kids are doing pretty well in most areas of their studies but get a bad grade in one class, we zoom in on the grade that needs to be improved. We soon see all of life through these negative, it's-gotta-be-fixed lenses, and our emotions and physiology fall in line with them. We think this is reality, what our world really looks like. But it isn't. Prayer restores our focus on who and what is actually real.

> **When anxiety knocks at the door of your heart, let prayer answer it.**

When anxiety knocks at the door of your heart, let prayer answer it. Right from the start, acknowledge that your Father is the God who can deal with the situation, whatever it happens to be. He can heal cancers or carry you through seasons of grief. He can handle your unemployment and find you a new job—probably His purpose all along, even if the process felt traumatic to you. He can get into the heart of the child who isn't following Him, and He may have ways of doing it that you haven't even considered yet. Look at the universe He created and recognize whom you're praying to. Nothing is too difficult for Him (Jeremiah 32:27). Nothing going on in your life is bigger than He is.

Most of us know that intellectually. But we don't experience it until we worship Him. We have to pause, reflect, and pray for it to begin to sink into our hearts. The first word Paul uses for prayer takes us to that place of worship and adoration that gives us a true perspective.

● *Petition*

The second most common word in the New Testament for prayer focuses on need. It's a prayer that expresses need before we ask, a sense that we're unable to handle what we're facing. We know we have limitations, and we know God doesn't. Our impulse to petition Him comes from this acute awareness that we need Him.

That's where many of our anxieties come from, in fact. We face a problem or concern, and we immediately wonder how we're going to respond, what we're going to do to fix it, how we will be able to cope. The more we think those thoughts, the more overwhelmed we begin to feel. Our sense of need just grows and grows.

If the first kind of prayer turns us in the direction of adoration, this one turns us toward confession. *God, I can't handle this situation. I don't know what to do. I have tried everything under the sun. Unless You intervene, I don't know how I'll get by* . . . It doesn't matter whether this is about a marriage crisis, a rebellious child, a difficult boss, a financial disaster, or anywhere else you feel like you're in over your head. Certain situations in life will drive us to our knees, and we feel like we have no other option than to plead for help. That's more than okay. Paul actually recommends this kind of prayer for just these anxiety-producing moments.

These situations bring us to a place of humility and dependency. We can't cast our cares on God while we're still holding on to them, somehow thinking we might still be able to handle them with our hard work, ingenuity, personality, and creativity. We like to be problem-solvers. But when we encounter problems we can't solve, we have to humble ourselves and acknowledge our dependence on God. Our petitions grow out of that attitude.

> **We can't cast our cares on God while we're still holding on to them.**

When we bring our petitions to God, we are essentially saying, "Lord, I know You care for me. I can't handle this, but You can." That confession—that focus on our needs—positions us to ask Him for help.

● *Thanksgiving*

This is an interesting compound word in Greek. It comes from several roots that together include the ideas of rejoicing, being glad, showing favor, and having grace. Gratitude is not just an expression of prayer, it's an attitude that should liberally season every other kind of prayer. It's a focus on and appreciation for what God has done.

This is a natural outcome of the first two types of prayer we looked at. When I'm looking up at the stars and worshiping God, or I'm confessing how incapable I am of handling the challenges I'm facing, He very often reminds me of how good He has been in the past—how Theresa and I have made it through so many things in four decades of marriage, how my son was in ICU and got well, or the impossible situations I've been in that turned out not to be impossible when God got involved. And I say, "Thank You." He has been faithful. That awareness needs to saturate all our prayers.

If your mind wanders when you pray, if you have trouble concentrating and staying focused, you may find that your prayers and petitions aren't really getting rid of your anxiety. You spend time talking to God, but your mind is here and there and everywhere, and by the time you're done, the anxieties are exactly where they were before. I can certainly relate to that. But I've learned that anxiety can't coexist with thankfulness. The two really just don't go together. Your petitions, as important as they are, are still very often focused on your problems and needs. Thanksgiving is focused on the good things God has filled your life with. In the fullness of biblical prayer, when we add gratitude to our prayers and petitions, anxiety eventually gives way.

Anxiety can't coexist with thankfulness.

For example, I sometimes have trouble concentrating during difficult times. I pray, remind myself of who God is, confess what I am not able to do, and ask for a renewed mind and forgiveness for self-focus. But I still may be looking at things through a negative lens and having negative emotions. Sometimes my mind wanders—you've probably experienced how unfocused we can be when we're praying and get distracted with pressing thoughts—so I've learned to make a list. I keep a journal and write down things I'm thankful for, then I go through them one by one.

Nothing is too big or small to put on this list. I've thanked God for times of rest, laughing with Theresa, hearing her say she felt better physically than she had in a long time, enjoying many of the gifts He has put in my life, appreciating that I haven't had to take anti-inflammatories for my surgically repaired back in several days, the encouragement He has given me, the opportunities to help other people I meet, and on and on with everything that comes to mind. In spite of all the unpleasantness and difficulties of many aspects of life, in spite of personal shortcomings and mistakes as a husband, father, leader, and friend, I can thank God for loving me, delighting in me, having mercy on me and my family, and giving me a fruitful ministry. He isn't shocked by the fact that I don't measure up, by my limitations, or by my need of His mercy and grace every moment of every day.

By the time I get through recognizing all those things I'm thankful for—His provision, protection, guidance, and grace—I am at peace. Anxiety is gone. I'm not worried about not measuring up, being overwhelmed, and not being able to handle the difficulties well. Just being honest about those things prompts gratitude. I have great needs, but I also have a great God. And thanking Him helps me experience His presence, where no anxiety can stand.

Requests

This last word is powerful. What do you do in light of your adoration, confession, and thanksgiving? After you have worshiped God for who He is, seen your need, and focused on what He has already done, what's next? You outline your needs and make requests.

This is where we get specific. Many people don't experience God's peace and power because they pray general prayers—that God would help them grow spiritually, bless their family, help their children, and work things out for a good day. That's like Theresa sending me to the store and telling me to buy some good food she knows how to cook and that everyone will like. She just wouldn't do that. She would give me a list, take a picture of the label, remind me it has to be organic or the sixteen-ounce size or low-sodium—everything down to the detail. We go to the store to get specific things.

Or imagine asking a ten-year-old what he or she wants for Christmas and hearing, "Oh, I don't know. Just some good stuff. You know what's best." That's not usually how it works, is it? Even at a young age, we have a strong sense of what we need and want, and we don't hesitate to ask for it.

God is much more than a store or a Santa Claus, and we don't ever want to treat Him like a heavenly vending machine. But He is our source for everything, and He does encourage us to make specific requests. I write specific things in my journal and put a check-box next to them, just like a grocery list. When I pray, I give them to the God who is all-wise, all-powerful, and all-loving. I turn my cares, concerns, and anxieties into requests. When He answers, I check them off. As I write this, I have a list that is just a few weeks old, but only two unchecked boxes remain. I'm experiencing that God is showing up. He's alive in my life. He's alive in yours too, but if you aren't asking specifically and in some way tracking the answers, you may not be aware of it.

We are invited to pray for definite things. *God, I ask You specifically to move in my supervisor's heart to give me favor with him and for me to make a significant contribution in this meeting. Lord, I'm asking You for "x" amount of dollars because this is what is happening in our family situation, and this is what we need to deal with it. God, I am asking You for the best doctor in this region. Help me find the right one. Will You set up the right contacts so we can deal with this cancer?*

Once you've worshiped God for who He is, acknowledged your need, and thanked Him for how He has been gracious to you, you can tell Him what you want. Give Him the "grocery list." Some people do only that, and they come across as demanding and entitled. But your previous three kinds of prayer have worked the right attitude into your heart, and you are invited to come boldly to God and ask. You're His son or daughter, and He wants to help you.

I try to turn all my anxieties into prayers. When an anxious thought comes, I try to see it not as a threat or stressor but as a prayer prompt. Writing them down and checking them off helps me in the mental process of giving it to God, and I know I can trust Him to handle it in just the right way. Some requests take time, but it isn't because God is hard of hearing or slow about His answers. He's a master of timing. But I can see over time that He is alive in my life. He shows up in amazing ways. If you pray specifically and track your prayers, you'll see Him showing up in your life too.

You are invited to come boldly to God and ask.

If you've had children, you've probably had the experience of your child having a bad dream, running into your bedroom, and asking to get in the bed with you. You open the covers and let them in, and thirty seconds later they are sound asleep and breathing deeply. Why? They have gotten close to the one who loves them, is in control, and can protect them. They have found refuge in a safe place.

That's what the God of the universe is inviting you, His child, to do. He wants you to stop fretting, stop trying to figure out how you can solve everything, and get close to Him. He wants you to see His arms around you and begin breathing deeply and resting soundly again. He wants you to pray this kind of prayer—adoration, confession, thanksgiving, and supplication—and run into His arms.

Why We Pray: The Promise of Peace

Philippians 4:7 promises that "the peace of God, which transcends all understanding, will guard your hearts and your minds in Christ Jesus." This would be an empty promise if the prayers of the previous verse were not powerful in transforming us and the circumstances around us. But because these kinds of prayers lead to this kind of peace, we can draw some very important, logical conclusions:

1. Peace and anxiety cannot coexist.
2. Anxiety and biblical prayer cannot coexist.

This is the promise of these two verses and the reason we pray. Anxiety really does give way to the peace of God.

One way to put the step-by-step process of this chapter into memorable form is to think of ACTS. *A* is the adoration of our prayer; *C* is the confession implied in our petition; *T* is thanksgiving; and *S* is our supplication, the requests we actually ask for. As soon as anxiety knocks at your door, remember ACTS and run into your Father's arms—again and again and again.

> **A**-Adoration
> **C**-Confession
> **T**-Thanksgiving
> **S**-Supplication

Don't be alarmed if this takes some practice. You don't go out on a golf course two or three times a year and expect to make par on every hole or go bowling for the first time in ten years and expect to score a 300. This is not magic. It's a spiritual mindset and practice we have to learn to develop in our lives. We do find some immediate relief, but we also get better at it over time.

We have all developed lifelong patterns in our thought life and habitual responses to the anxieties we feel. Many of us have unintentionally cultivated some very dysfunctional, painful, damaging ways of dealing with worries and stress that are bad for ourselves, our relationship with God, our family members and friends, and our work. If that's true for you, this is going to take some persistence. Thought patterns don't change immediately; in fact, they usually take at least three weeks to begin to change, and even then, the old neural pathways battle against the new neural pathways for supremacy. So you'll have to go into training and be tenacious about it.

You'll have to go into training and be tenacious about change.

If you're in the middle of a stressful situation and need to walk through this process of prayer, it's okay to take a break. I've been in anxious situations and not known what to do next, and I've just excused myself to step out of the room so I could have a few minutes with God. I ask Him to help me remember the steps, I acknowledge His abilities and my limitations, thank Him throughout the whole conversation, and tell Him I need His wisdom, power, and love in that moment. He gives His peace even in times like that. He is more than willing to meet us in our times of need.

Remember, biblical prayer is God's antidote to anxiety. It's simple and profound. Whenever you feel anxious, even in the coming hours, days, and weeks, remember ACTS. When anxiety pounds on the door of your heart, let prayer answer it as you run into your Father's arms.

This promise is for those who have entered into a relationship with Jesus. If God is not yet your Father—if you haven't yet become His child by faith—this won't work. If that describes you, the first prayer is easy: choose today to ask Him in. Receive Him by faith. It's the biggest, most effective anxiety-relieving prayer you could ever pray. When you turn from your self-will and sin and ask Him to forgive you and take up residence inside you, your peace begins. And for the rest of your life, no matter how many stressful situations you find yourself in, you will have everything

Biblical prayer is God's antidote to anxiety.

you need for the peace of God to guard your heart and mind in Christ. All His children are welcome at any moment to run into His arms to find peace.

QUESTIONS FOR DISCUSSION AND REFLECTION

1. When do you tend to be anxious? What situations or people bring out your stress? How can you prepare spiritually to handle those stresses?

2. What issues in your life are "strangling" and "stressing" you mentally and emotionally? What would your life be like if you cast those cares on God and released them?

3. In what ways will you put the message of this chapter into practice? Who will help/encourage you in your battle to overcome anxiety?

4. Do you know of someone in your network of relationships who would benefit from this pattern of prayer? How can you share this with someone else who struggles with anxiety and needs your help?

CHAPTER 3

Choose Peace
in a Broken World

What is your greatest fear right now? I'm not talking about passing thoughts or today's momentary troubles. Those come and go without causing too much stress in our hearts and minds. I'm asking what you fear most in this season of life. Are you afraid of the future? Something bad happening to one of your kids? The economy? Never getting married? A health issue? The direction of the world? Several of those or something like them may surface in your worries at times, but most people have one in particular that weighs on them consistently. What ties your stomach in knots or raises your heart rate when you think about it? What keeps you awake at night or makes it to the top of your prayer list every time you pray?

Now think about what it would be like to overcome that fear—not necessarily to make the situation go away, but to be able to think about it without any worry or anxiety. Imagine how different your life would be. What would it feel like to be free?

It would take some effort, of course. Lasting change in anything, including our spiritual lives, isn't easy. But it is possible. We've seen that in Jesus's promise to His disciples to give them His peace (John 14:27). It's also in Isaiah's prophecy that God will keep in perfect peace those whose minds are steadfastly trusting in Him (Isaiah 26:3). The most common command in all of Scripture is to not be afraid—often followed with, "Because I am with you." We apparently have to be told this very often, with many promises and reassurances. But because we are told so persistently and repeatedly, we know it's possible. It's something God enables us to do.

How do we experience God's power and presence to the degree that our awareness of Him undoes our fear in the midst of storms? How do we get free from the fear that seems to enslave so many of us? In order to answer those questions, we first need to understand how God has wired us—how our mind and emotions work together. That will tell us a lot about how to deal with living fearlessly in a broken world.

A study conducted at the University of Tennessee several years ago divided participants into two groups—one that listened to a radio program with benign news for five minutes every day for twelve years, and another that listened to a program with negative news for the same time. The group listening to negative news heard about earthquakes, crimes, abductions, riots, scams, murders, and all the other things the rest of us hear about from time to time, but they were required to hear concentrated segments of it every day. After twelve years, the two groups were evaluated. The people who listened to the negative news were more depressed, pessimistic, and afraid than the other group, and they were less likely to trust and help others.[1]

That's not particularly surprising, of course; it confirms what many of us would have suspected. But the fact that this exposure to negative news was only five minutes a day over and above what people normally hear rather than a three-hour scary movie every day is sobering. It tells us that even small adjustments to our mental and emotional diet can have major effects.

The familiar phrase, "You are what you eat," is not just true about our physical bodies, is it? If we eat lots of sweets and fats, we end up a lot larger and less healthy than if we eat lots of fruits and vegetables. But we are what we eat psychologically too. Science and Scripture fully agree on this point: Whatever we keep taking in will work its way into our hearts and minds and have substantial impact on what we think and how we feel.

We can't eliminate the bad things that happen in the world. A lot of challenging circumstances are going on out there at any given moment. That's reality. But how we handle them makes a difference. If we keep feeding our fears, they will grow stronger. We have to learn to starve our fear and feed our faith.

The Truth about Our Thoughts and Feelings

Science and Scripture are in sync on the effects of our thinking on the rest of our lives. Studies like the one mentioned above confirm many truths from the Bible, including these three:

1. We are the products of our thought lives. You are who you are today because of the things you've thought in the past. Those things shaped your opinions, attitudes, decisions, and beliefs. "As he thinketh in his heart, so is he," says the old King James translation of Proverbs 23:7. You live out the thoughts you entertain. You follow the form shaped in your heart. Or, as is often said, you become what you behold.

2. Our emotions flow from our thoughts. Whatever you think triggers feelings about that thought. Sometimes this process is hardly noticeable; you can find yourself feeling a certain way without realizing how you got there. But your thoughts shape your emotions, and you make decisions based on the emotions that have followed your thoughts. Romans 8:6 tells us that "the mind governed by the flesh is death, but the mind governed by the Spirit is life and peace." When the Holy Spirit shapes our thoughts, our hearts are at peace.

3. What we allow into our minds is the most important decision we make each day. If your thoughts shape who you are and how you feel, then what you feed your thoughts with becomes an extremely important series of choices. For better or worse, what you watch, listen to, read, say, and think about are life changing. Your eyes and ears are the gateways of your soul, and whatever enters in will seep down and color your perspective of everything. Over time, those seemingly minor choices add up to a personality, a philosophy of life, a belief system, or however else you might describe your mental and emotional makeup.

When the Holy Spirit shapes our thoughts, our hearts are at peace.

That ought to give every parent pause. You have an obligation to care for not only your own mental and emotional state but also that of your children. If you have kids in your house, you need to find loving and respectful ways to be a gatekeeper for their eyes and ears. It isn't easy today with the access children have to videos and music through their phones, laptops, and other devices. But there's a world out there competing to capture your children's hearts, and they don't suspect a thing. They tend to let anything in when they are young, and even when they are older and more discerning, they can get caught in tempting and deceptive images and ideas. They need you to train them in filtering out the harmful influences that will affect their personalities, perspectives, and beliefs.

These three truths have obvious relevance to our fears. If we are the product of our thoughts, our emotions flow from our thoughts, and our mental and emotional intake is such an important decision each moment of the day, we very clearly have the ability to feed our fears or starve them. They are the product of what we've been fed, and that's an area where we have a lot of control. So we have to change our psychological "diet" in order to weaken fear and strengthen faith.

How Can We Choose Peace in a Broken World?

When Paul wrote his letter to the Philippians, he had been going through some very challenging experiences for several years. He had been arrested on false charges, confined for at least a couple of years, brought before local rulers, taken on a ship to Rome, and then placed under house arrest awaiting an official trial. That's where he was at the time of this letter, yet he had peace. And he wanted the Philippians to have the same kind of peace in the circumstances they were facing.

The Roman world was filled with violence and injustice, and Christians often felt those injustices acutely. They were very aware that they lived in a broken world. We can relate— perhaps not to the same kinds of injustices they experienced, but certainly to that strong awareness of the brokenness all around us. So Paul's words are as relevant to us as they were to the people of Philippi two millennia ago, and they assure us that we can have peace in an uncertain world. They also tell us how.

> Finally, brothers and sisters, whatever is true, whatever is noble, whatever is right, whatever is pure, whatever is lovely, whatever is admirable—if anything is excellent or praiseworthy—think about such things. (Philippians 4:8)

This is our mental agenda, the things we should fill our minds with all the time. Paul is saying that of all the different ways to think about life, this is God's way. We are to let our minds dwell on these things, to ponder, meditate, review, and become saturated in them.

But he immediately follows this command with a second one: "Whatever you have learned or received or heard from me, or seen in me—put it into practice" (Philippians 4:9). He reminds them of the things they learned when he was with them—the things they hungered for, took in, and actually applied. They heard him talk and watched him live, and he now calls them to follow that lifestyle. This is how Paul nurtured his own thought life.

And then comes the promise: "And the God of peace will be with you" (v. 9). In other words, the God of *shalom*, the Father of blessing and favor, the one who protects and provides and wants to give us the best in life, will do more than give us peace. He will be with us.

> **Command #1:** Think about these things.
>
> **Command #2:** Put this into practice.
>
> **The Promise:** The God of peace will be with you.

We are all a product of our thoughts, yet most of us can be extremely casual with what we allow into our minds. We are shaping our character, decisions, perspectives, beliefs, and emotions without really paying attention to what we are shaping them with. That's a serious problem.

So let's look at the words Paul uses to describe a godly, healthy thought life. For each one, I want us to look at a definition and a question that will help us discern what we are feeding our minds. If you were to ask these questions for ninety days before you let anything through your eyes and ears into your heart and mind, or before you let the harmful thoughts and feelings that are already in there grow deeper and stronger roots, you would be shocked at the improvement in your emotional health. The lies, fears, insecurities, and everything else that disturbs your soul would stop undermining your faith and disrupting your peace. Your life will change dramatically.

The first command in these two verses tells us to think about these things—to dwell on them, contemplate them deeply, meditate on them, talk about them, ponder them, and let them sink in. The word is *logizomai*, literally to reckon, consider, keep a mental record, and to reason about. We get *logic* from this word, not because it implies unemotional, detached rationalism but because it suggests our normal process of reasoning and deducing. That's how we discern good and evil and decide what we're going to fix our minds on and what we'll filter out. Paul tells us to line up that mental process with reality and use it to our advantage.

● *Whatever Is True*

We are constantly confronted with lies. Some of them come from outside of us; others are thoughts, perceptions, and impressions we have developed deep inside over the years. Sometimes they are overt; others are subtle and hard to put a finger on. We are constantly exposed to misleading thoughts and become so accustomed to them that we rarely stop to ask if they are actually true.

I woke up one morning recently with a negative attitude. I don't know where it came from. I just saw everything through a negative lens. So I put this verse into practice. I prayed slowly through Psalm 23 and began to see things a little more positively—until I remembered that I needed to do my back exercises, which I don't exactly enjoy. As that bad attitude was creeping back in, I decided to say out loud every verse that came to mind during my exercises. I quoted passage after passage, which I can count on as truth, and then started declaring things about myself that I know to be true: *I'm a son of the living God. I have an inheritance in Him. He is preparing a place for me in heaven. He has given me spiritual gifts and has filled my heart with His peace. He has blessed me with a wonderful wife and children who love me.* On and on, I declared these things out loud, and little by little I was filled with gratitude. My negative emotions faded away.

We tend to believe a lot of lies and premises from early in life. In *The 4:8 Principle,* a book focused entirely on this one verse from the Bible, Tommy Newberry lists many of the things we unconsciously tell ourselves that produce negative emotions, including anxiety and fear.[2] We make inner vows or assumptions: *I'll never be happy again, things probably won't work out for me, bad things always happen to me, I'm not worthy of being loved, I just have to accept my limitations, I never say the right thing, I'm not attractive, funny, interesting, smart . . .* You get the idea. Each of us has something like this going on inside us, and we may not even realize it. It's our "normal." But it isn't true.

Since you're the product of your thought life, these kinds of inner assumptions tend to prove true over time. We live out the things we believe. If we want anything to change in our lives, we have to learn to think differently.

If this sounds like positive thinking, you're right. It is—at least in the sense that God's truth about you is very positive, and He tells you to agree with it and let your mind dwell on it. But it isn't *only* positive thinking. Usually when people criticize that concept, they assume it means talking ourselves into something that isn't true. But in this case, we're talking ourselves into something that *is* true. We're leaving behind the lies that have done nothing but harm us and embracing what God says. And He is very positive about His love for you and who you are in Him.

If we want anything to change in our lives, we have to learn to think differently.

Some of the lies we believe are hard to pinpoint because they are mixed with truth—for example, the idea that our children's education and career choices are evidence of whether we succeeded or failed as parents. Are you really a failure if your son or daughter doesn't get into the best school and become a doctor or lawyer? Does your reputation really depend on such things? These thoughts come from insecurity and produce anxiety. They also create pressure on your children and other people around you and produce unhealthy, dysfunctional side effects. They are good aspirations attached to faulty reasoning. Wanting your children to do well is a desire based on truth. Defining success for them and tying it to your own self-perception is a lie.

Another lie is the idea that you will never be happy unless . . . you get married, own your own home, have the right job, or whatever else you want to finish the sentence with. This is not a true premise. You may long for one of these things, and there's nothing wrong with having the desire, but the idea that you will be miserable and unfulfilled without it is a lie.

The lies we believe are hard to pinpoint because they are mixed with truth.

This is what we call "premise thinking"— the idea that some activity, success, event, or person will make things right for you. If this happens, then you'll be happy. Otherwise, you won't. That's a false belief.

These desires are not bad, of course, but there's a big difference between thinking it would be nice for them to be satisfied and thinking that satisfying them is necessary for you to have value or be fulfilled as a person. None of these things are promised in Scripture as the key to fulfillment or a statement of your value as a human being. Your value is not dependent on grades, athletic success, career advancement, a marriage and family situation, a home, a lifestyle, or anything other than God's view of you. You are loved by Him, adopted into His family, sealed with His Spirit, and given a purpose of glorifying Him with your life. That's the truth. Any deviation from that truth is a lie.

When we dwell on what is true, we are choosing to focus on objective reality according to God. We reject distortions, deviations, and deceptions. We refuse to embrace illusions that promise peace and happiness but can't ultimately deliver.

We think about and meditate on the reality of what God says.

The question to ask on this point when you're discerning what to let into your mind is very straightforward: *Is this true or false?* That is not at all the same as asking whether something *looks* true or false. It's a question that digs down into the truth or falsehood of our perspectives.

Your emotions, after all, are not necessarily responses to reality. They are responses to your *perception* of reality. The people who listened to negative news in the study mentioned above developed a different perception of reality over time than their counterparts who listened to benign news. They more often assumed that other people wanted to harm them, that disaster was more likely to happen, or that disease was more likely to affect them. Their perceptions lined up with stories of what had actually happened in the world but didn't fit the likelihood or statistical probabilities of what might happen. Their sense of reality was skewed toward the negative.

All of us have experienced this distinction between reality and perception. You might see something that looks like a snake, and instantly you freeze: your heart rate accelerates, your stomach tightens, and you experience a jolt of adrenaline. Then you look closer and discover it was just a coiled rope or twisted branch, and everything in you calms back down. You just experienced an emotional response to your perception, not to what actually existed. But the emotions were exactly the same as if you had really seen a snake.

Human beings engage in a lot of "snake" thinking—fears, worries, anxieties, dread, and panic that profoundly affect our emotional state even when based on something that isn't actually true. In every situation in life, ask yourself, *Is this true or false?* Then let your mind dwell on whatever is true.

Whatever Is Noble

This word, often translated *honorable*, means sober, serious, worthy of respect, inspiring awe. It refers to those things in our lives that reflect the weight and importance of our purpose. Nothing is wrong with getting excited about a basketball game, awards programs, a fantasy football league, or a great new movie. But these are peripheral to our lives. The world is full of trivia, and in the midst of it all, we have been given a serious, sobering mission full of eternal meaning and significance. We have been rescued from eternal condemnation through the amazing gift of the sacrifice of God's Son on a cross. We are loved unconditionally, live under the umbrella of His favor, and walk out His amazing plan for our lives. We are God's workmanship (Ephesians 2:10), His artistry and poetry, designed for a purpose He specifically ordained for us from before the foundation of the world. That's a big deal. It's honorable and noble.

Are you fulfilling that purpose? That's a weighty issue. You are living in a small window of time but have been created for eternity. Heaven and hell are real. You are called to live simultaneously in overflowing joy and in the sobering reality of your calling. You don't need to focus on that all the time and carry a serious expression on your face into every joyful situation, but do not buy into the fast-paced, pleasure-above-all culture we live in. The writer of Ecclesiastes says there is far more wisdom at a funeral than at a party (7:2). Let those deep thoughts shape your perspective.

Theresa once asked me what I'm most afraid of. I said, "Squandering the life God has given me and falling short of His purpose for me."

"Why?" she asked.

"Because at least by the world's standards, I'm more successful than I thought I would be, and God has given us more than I dreamed of. But that can create a lifestyle and comfort level that work against the kind of focus and sacrifice I need to have in taking up my cross and following Him. I don't want to slip into a status-quo life that everyone else thinks is wonderful, but I and the Lord both know better."

That's a noble thought, and I've had to be intentional about keeping it in front of me. It doesn't just happen when we let our minds wander. We have to choose to fix our minds on whatever is honorable.

So ask this question about the things you let into your mind: *Does this honor or dishonor God?* That's a broad question that applies to His nature and character, His purposes and calling for our lives, and the eternity He has set before us. When you're watching or listening to something, when you're engaged in a relationship or an activity, does it honor Him? Is it noble? Is it a gray area that isn't necessarily evil but also not particularly uplifting? Or does it clearly glorify

Him and align with His ways? Let your mind think about the things that are noble and honorable.

● Whatever Is Right

This word is also translated as *righteous*. In the New Testament, it refers to God's actions and His character and describes the life of Jesus. It pictures doing the right thing when tempted. Another way we might interpret it is living with integrity.

God's character creates a standard, and integrity for a Christian means aligning with that standard. It is not outside of Him as a universal norm or ideal that even He conforms to. It's the ideal that is in Him and that the rest of the universe should conform to.

The question you need to ask here is, *Is this right or wrong? Is it the whole truth or a partial truth?* Am I doing my taxes this way because it's what everyone else does or because it's the right thing to do? Am I fudging on this because I know I can get away with it or can justify it as ethical by my own definition? Is this a lack of integrity? Am I treating people right or defrauding someone? Is it okay to live with someone I'm "practically married" to? Does this video game honor life and love or do fictional people get blown up and mutilated by the fingers and thumbs of my kids? Are we just doing something recreational, or is it one of those many shades of gray?

These aren't always easy questions to answer. Some of them really are borderline issues that might be truly ethical and right from our own perspective but shady or wrong from someone else's. The Bible doesn't always give us black-and-white answers for everything. But it does tell us a lot about God's nature and character, and it calls us to conform to His ways. Use that as your standard. Then let your mind dwell on the things that are right.

● *Whatever Is Pure*

This word comes from the same root as *holy*—being "set apart" for a special purpose. It suggests being innocent, free from defilement and immorality in thought, word, and deed. When David said he had committed to live a blameless life and not set any vile thing before his eyes (Psalm 101:2–3), and when Job said he had made a covenant with his eyes not to gaze lustfully at a woman (Job 31:1), this is what they were talking about. We are called to turn our attention to things that are pure and not let ourselves be corrupted with impurity.

Here is the question we need to ask about the things we see and hear and think about: *Will this cleanse my soul or dirty it?* This applies not only to sexual issues but to any kind of immoral thought or behavior. But many people do tend to think of sex first when they think of biblical purity, and there's a good reason for that. It's one of the areas in which our culture has become particularly impure.

Studies show that some sexual sin is as addictive as cocaine, and trying hard to quit—getting rid of a porn addiction, for example—is almost impossible to do on your own. It's a pseudo-intimacy that will eventually destroy your relationships. It multiplies fears and creates the need to cover things up. God wants you to see sex as holy and pure because that's how He made it. He loves it and wants the marriage bed to be holy, set apart for that special purpose. Anything outside of that purpose is impure, and if that's an issue you struggle with, I strongly encourage you to get help. I've counseled countless men over the years who privately lived with a secret porn addiction that was destroying their souls. Years of duplicity, shame, guilt, and fear of being found out strangled their intimacy with God and often their intimacy with their spouse. God wants so much better for us.

But pornography isn't the only sexual impurity our culture deals with. It's only the most obvious. Some are much more subtle, like movies that blur the lines between right and wrong and turn our sympathies in opposite directions. You've probably seen plots like these—a woman is married to a really self-centered, unappealing jerk of a husband and falls in love with a likable, selfless guy who seems just right for her. We find ourselves rooting against that marriage, don't we? Her affair doesn't bother us; we just want her to find true love. And all of a sudden, we've been sucked into one of the enemy's strategies for skewing our morals and making impurity look pure.

> **The battle for our lives is not out there in the world. It's in our hearts and minds.**

The battle for our lives is not out there in the world. It's in our hearts and minds. The weapons of our warfare are not fleshly but powerful for pulling down spiritual strongholds. We need to take every thought captive and make it obedient to Christ (2 Corinthians 10:3–5). Have conversations with your children about what's going into their minds and, without any judgment, find out where you can help. Examine your own filters too. Ask yourself if the things you take in are cleansing or corrupting. Let your mind dwell on whatever is pure.

● Whatever Is Lovely

This word refers to things that are attractive, winsome, and beautiful. It's a wonderful word that calls for a response of love and warmth rather than bitterness, criticism, and vengeance. It urges us to smell the roses, look at rainbows, watch kids playing in the park, think about pleasant memories, read or watch something encouraging, and enjoy the pleasant things God has put into our world. It calls us to notice good things.

I found myself driving at about 6:30 one morning recently and noticed the red-and-pink sky behind the puffy clouds in front of me. It was beautiful—one of those moments that makes you think, *Oh, Lord, that's just amazing.* I had been listening to songs on my phone, shuffled so that they come up randomly. And the one that came on in that moment was written by a young man who was one of my son's best friends. He died of cancer at twenty-five, and his song, "Restore Me," brought back a flood of memories of what God had done and how He orchestrates our lives and walks with us through our joys and our pains. It softened my heart and made me appreciate the beauty all around me—the ocean and the redwoods, the clouds and the colors of the sun against the sky, things we don't always appreciate when our faces are glued to a screen.

By contrast, when I got home later that day and turned on the news, the stories of violence and murder were disturbing. I flipped to a PBS channel, which often plays encouraging documentaries, and the program airing then was disturbing too. Within ten minutes, I had gone from a glorious moment to sadness and anger about all the injustices in this messed-up world. Everything that was on my screen went into my heart and completely changed my thoughts and feelings.

So the question to ask about things that are lovely is, *Will this renew my heart or harden it?* We don't need to stick our heads in the sand and avoid every hint of bad news, but we do need balance, and news programs are not going to give it to us. They give us constantly flowing streams of everything that's wrong, and very occasionally something that is right. Meanwhile, hundreds of millions of acts of kindness are happening all around us. Children are being welcomed into the world, people are being generous and loving, people in need are being reached with food and fresh water, women are being rescued from the sex trade. Yes, there's a sex trade to begin with, and yes, people are hungry and thirsty. But many people focus only on those tragedies and completely miss all the wonderful things going on too. Choosing not to dwell on whatever isn't lovely is healthy. We're aware of those things, but we are not meant to fixate on them.

What you allow into your mind the first and last thirty to forty-five minutes of your day will shape your subconscious thoughts. You either starve your fear and feed your faith or do the opposite. Make sure you are choosing to think about things that are lovely.

Whatever Is Admirable

Paul then adds the idea of thinking of things that are commendable, of good reputation, gracious. *Admirable* literally means fair spoken or well reported. It describes things that are fit for God to hear rather than false, ugly, impure words that do not line up with who He is. Paul follows this word, and really the whole list, with the clarifying words *excellent* and *praiseworthy*. We are to turn our minds toward whatever is virtuous, wholesome, and good.

Here's the question to ask with this instruction: *Can I recommend this to someone who looks up to me?* That's a sobering thought, but it's an important one. If you've ever been watching something and felt the need to change the channel before someone else walked in the room; if you've ever modified your behavior because you want to present the right face to someone else; if you've ever had to clean up your words or actions because impressionable people are watching, then you have a sense of what this instruction is about.

Imagine sitting on your couch watching something on your TV, phone, or laptop, and the resurrected Jesus walks in and sits down next to you. "May I join you?" He asks.

Obviously, you say yes.

Now, how comfortable are you with His presence, with Him seeing what you see, knowing what you think? And how comfortable would you be with Him looking on while you allow others in your household, even young children, to see what you're seeing? What would He say about what your habits are doing to your own heart and mind, and what would He say about how those habits are affecting others? If you are the representation of Jesus to other people around you— young children or people new in the faith—what impression are they getting? Can you recommend this movie, this scene, this conversation to them? Is it admirable?

If you're like me, you've had the sobering thought that if some people look up to you as the model Christian, that's not a good situation to be in for either of us. But people do. If you are a follower of Jesus, to many people you are a representative of Jesus. The song many of us have sung to our children, "Be Careful Little Eyes What You See," is good advice for us too. Not because God is looking down in judgment but, as the song says, because He is looking down in love. He wants the best for us.

Matt Maher and my son, Jason Ingram, wrote a song based on Zephaniah 3:17 that begins with the line, "I flirt with the world, it steals my love for you."[3] It goes on to talk about how God delights in His children and sings over us. There is nothing condemning in that thought. It expresses the heart of a Father who wants to protect us from harm and help us find our satisfaction in Him.

When we put things in our minds that distance us from our Father's nature and character, we are driving a wedge in the relationship. He is not withdrawing His love from us—He never does that—but our fellowship with Him suffers. We stop sensing His presence and experiencing His love as we should. Guilt and shame keep us from drawing close to Him, even though drawing close is exactly what we need when we feel guilt and shame.

If you need help for a problem with pornography, violence, or other destructive and addictive thoughts, plenty of ministries and caring friends can help you plug into accountability groups, offer wise counsel, and encourage you with grace-filled conversations. You will never find yourself "too far gone," "too late," or "too" anything for God's help. But whatever you do, cultivate your connection with the Father. Saturate your mind with God-filled thoughts.

Saturate your mind with God-filled thoughts.

This is not just a call to a superspiritual mindset. Just read, listen to, watch, and think about healthy things. I recently finished listening to an audio book on the life of Winston Churchill, and the ways he responded with courage to things happening in the war, though not necessarily "spiritual," were certainly admirable, noble, and worthy of praise. I read a book on the life of Martin Luther and was inspired by many of his actions. Some of the things I read and listen to are about faith and Christian experiences, but others are about the beauty and truth God has woven into the world.

The statistics for depression and anxiety in our country and our world are alarming, especially among teens, and much of the problem is what people think about. If we're the product of our thought life, it only makes sense to fill our lives with good things. Paul's categories of thought cover a lot of territory—anything with moral excellence that will inspire us and motivate us to love God and others. Think about such things. New mental habits are life changing.

Put It into Practice

The point, Paul says, is not just to know about these things and agree that they are good. It's to put them into practice. That's what he says in verse 9, pointing to his own habits and practices as an example: "Whatever you have learned or received or heard from me, or seen in me." He is essentially telling them that their appetite for truth and their application of it (what they have learned and received) and the instruction and modeling they have seen in him are prompts for an ongoing lifestyle. His instruction to put these things into practice does not point to a onetime event. It's a lasting, habitual, ongoing life of thinking new things and living a new life.

Why is this important? Because *your thought life determines your future.* Whatever your hopes are, whatever dreams you've had, whatever calling you've sensed from God, all of it will be affected and even determined by the ways you think. Your passions and joys, your expectations for the kinds of friends and family you will have and the kind of work you will do, these

Your thought life determines your future.

forward-looking pictures are informed and shaped by your thought patterns today.

Paul addressed this dynamic in his letter to the Romans in pretty graphic terms, and I'm sharing it in the Amplified Version–Classic Edition (with implied meanings in brackets) because of how thoroughly it expresses his language:

> For those who are according to the flesh and are controlled by its unholy desires set their minds on and pursue those things which gratify the flesh, but those who are according to the Spirit and are controlled by the desires of the Spirit set their minds on and seek those things which gratify the [Holy] Spirit.
>
> Now the mind of the flesh [which is sense and reason without the Holy Spirit] is death [death that comprises all the miseries arising from sin, both here and hereafter]. But the mind of the [Holy] Spirit is life and [soul] peace [both now and forever].
>
> [That is] because the mind of the flesh [with its carnal thoughts and purposes] is hostile to God, for it does not submit itself to God's Law; indeed it cannot.
>
> So then those who are living the life of the flesh [catering to the appetites and impulses of their carnal nature] cannot please or satisfy God, or be acceptable to Him. (Romans 8:5–8 AMP-CE)

Did you notice how focused this passage is on our thought life? And that those who are catering to carnal appetites and impulses *cannot please God*? But that we are given an invitation here to let our minds be empowered and guided by the Holy Spirit, which leads to life and peace? We cannot keep putting unwholesome, untrue, impure things in our minds and also expect to walk out God's purposes for us. Transformation always begins with our thinking.

How do we accomplish this? Through the principle of a renewed mind:

> Do not be conformed to this world (this age), [fashioned after and adapted to its external, superficial customs], but be transformed (changed) by the [entire] renewal of your mind [by its new ideals and its new attitude], so that you may prove [for yourselves] what is the good and acceptable and perfect will of God, *even* the thing which is good and acceptable and perfect [in His sight for you]. (Romans 12:2 AMP-CE, italics added)

In other words, as we allow our minds to be renewed into new thought patterns and godly perspectives, the good and perfect will of God increasingly plays out in our lives.

Notice that this is not an overnight process. I've been a Christian for more than four decades and still have to be intentional about some of the most basic things I was learning in those early years after coming to Christ. But I've seen transformation in my life, in the lives of those I love, and in many I've spoken to over the years. I know this

Transformation always begins with our thinking.

works. I have witnessed God responding faithfully to every move toward Him and every effort to think in renewed ways.

I have a little card on top of my remote control. It asks the questions we've covered in this chapter. Before I watch, listen to, or spend time thinking about something, I remind myself to consider these questions: *Is this true? Does it honor God? Is it right or wrong? Will it cleanse or dirty my soul? Will it renew or harden my heart? Would I recommend it to someone who looks up to me?* And a final one that fits the overall passage: *Will it bring peace or fear into my life?*

What lies do you believe? What harmful attitudes or patterns have you adopted? What thoughts fall short of God's character? Whatever deceptions and distortions have become a part of your life, pray about and think through practical ways you can replace them with whatever is good and true. Don't condemn yourself, but do seek change—persistently. Fill your heart and mind with truth. One of the best things you can do for yourself and the people who care about you is to establish biblical filters for your thought life and literal filters on your devices to help you continually choose whatever is true, noble, right, pure, lovely, and admirable.

> **Filters for Your Thought Life**
>
> Is this true or false?
>
> Is this right or wrong?
>
> Will it cleanse my soul or dirty it?
>
> Will this renew my heart or harden it?
>
> Can I recommend this to someone who looks up to me?
>
> Will it bring peace or fear into my life?

Years ago, I realized I had been believing a lie for most of my life. This lie was much of the driving force behind my type A personality, the reason I always felt compelled to fill holes in my life. The lie was that I am a prisoner of the opinions of the important, influential people in my life.

Some might call it being a "people pleaser," which came from being the son of an alcoholic father and learning how to keep the peace all the time. But whatever the source, I would agonize when my best judgment and even direction from the Lord was different from people I respected. I thought disagreeing with someone would irreparably harm our relationship, so I created an unhealthy lifestyle of trying to please everyone. It was frustrating and challenging, and simply trying hard to change didn't work. I had to address the lie.

So I made some cards I could carry around with me to remind me of truth. On one side is the lie I believed: *People only love me if I prove my worth, please them, and agree with them.* On the other side is the truth: *People love me and are for me, and they want me to live a life of joy, rhythm, rest, and fruitfulness in all areas of my life. I am accepted, loved, and valued for who I am.* Whenever the lie pops up, I pull out the card, read the lie to expose it, and say, "Stop." Then I read the truth on the other side. I'm setting my mind on the Spirit, not on the flesh. I'm choosing to think on the things that are true, noble, right, pure, lovely, and admirable.

I would strongly encourage you to do that. If you commit to shifting your thoughts toward truth, you just might be shocked at what God does as you renew your mind. If you think it's a good idea but never actually act on it, nothing will change. If you just try harder without addressing the lies, little will change. But if you saturate your mind in truth, the lies eventually cannot remain. Your mind is renewed.

The Promise of Peace

The promise Paul declares after his instructions on changing how we think is this: "The God of peace will be with you." Remember, peace is *shalom*, a rich, full expression of God's goodness in every area of your life. You receive not only His peace but His blessing, power, presence, and provision. He wants to fulfill the desires of your heart.

That strikes at the heart of the biggest lie most of us will ever believe: that God is not for us, that He will not come through for us unless we measure up. The truth is that God is outlandishly on your side. He wants to fill your life with His goodness. He is always ready to forgive.

The truth is that God is outlandishly on your side.

"Lord, you are so good, so ready to forgive, so full of unfailing love for all who ask for your help" (Psalm 86:5 NLT). That's a picture of David turning his thoughts toward what is good and true, and I think we all need that perspective. Many of us, me included, are predisposed to think of God with His arms crossed and His toe tapping, as though He is disappointed that we haven't been quite good enough and is waiting for us to do better. It's a lie. Scripture gives us a completely different picture.

You can change the way you think about these things. You can overcome the lies that produce fears, anxieties, regrets, and other distorted perceptions. But it will require guarding your mind like never before, being diligent about what goes in and what is kept out. It may require some radical rearranging of the things that come into your house, onto your screens, into your own mind, and into the lives of your children or grandchildren. You will have to reorient your thought life and monitor the things that shape it.

If you need any advice on how to get started, here's a game plan I've found to be very useful:

Read: The Bible	10 minutes
Pray: Talk with God	7 minutes
Listen: Sit quietly and listen	3 minutes
Apply: A specific truth, e.g., serve someone	1 minute

I created a three-week video journey called "Daily Discipline with Chip" in which I show how to meet with God, hear His voice, and understand His Word. I never go more than ten minutes, and I ask you to invest another ten every day for those three weeks. It grew out of the "sheltering in place" situation when COVID-19 first hit. Of all the tools or teaching I've ever done, this had the greatest, most positive impact on people, as they learned not just to "have devotions" but to renew their mind and actually experience God's power and presence.

That's roughly twenty minutes a day of spending time with God, and if you follow this plan, I strongly believe God will show up in your life like never before. Your thoughts and emotions won't change overnight, but a process of change will begin. After a week, you'll probably notice a difference. In two or three weeks, that difference will be much more obvious. In a month, three months, maybe a year, you'll be astonished at how your thoughts have changed. Those insecurities, addictions, anger issues, coping mechanisms, or whatever your particular issues happen to be will shift into far healthier ways of thinking. You will begin to see a new you. And you'll be very aware that the God of *shalom*—of wholeness, fullness, completeness, goodness, and satisfaction—is with you.

QUESTIONS FOR DISCUSSION AND REFLECTION

1. How does our thought life affect our emotions?

2. How would you describe the quality of your thought life? What adjustments do you sense God would have you make in what you view, read, and think?

3. Why is habitual practice of the truth so vital if we are to experience God's peace? Why do inconsistencies and discrepancies in our integrity create stress and lack of peace in our lives?

4. What insight has God given you in this chapter to help you experience His peace in your life? How will you choose to cooperate with His process in your life? Who might be able to help you?

CHAPTER 4

Choose Peace
in Difficult Circumstances

When COVID-19 first spread around the world in the spring of 2020 and whole nations were sent home to shelter in place, many people discovered that their gods—the props they depended on to give them peace—had failed. The isolation and loss of security removed many of the distractions and coping mechanisms we tend to use to avoid our fundamental spiritual issues. It revealed the cracks in the "society of escape" we talked about in chapter 2. When our society was forced to slow its pace, addictions, domestic conflict, and depression increased. We had no sporting events or daily interactions at work or school to distract us. Fear over losing jobs, savings, and social opportunities crept in.

The world's discontentment became much more apparent under the spotlight of the pandemic.

Contentment may seem like a simple state of mind, but all it takes is a crisis to demonstrate how elusive it can be. Nearly every human being longs for that place where striving, struggling, and endless treadmills of trying to get ahead are no longer needed. We want to get past that feeling of everything we reach for being just beyond our grasp. We simply want to be content. And for most people, that means living beyond the turmoil of difficult circumstances.

Contentment is not about living beyond difficulties. It's about having peace in the midst of them. We can't be truly content unless we're anchored in something much greater than the trials and turmoil around us. Once we are, it really does become a simple concept. But "simple" and "easy" are not the same thing. For many people, that simple concept is extremely difficult to put into practice.

In our fallen nature, we are not very content beings. Part of that is by design; God has wired us to long for advances in our own spiritual growth and in the growth of His kingdom. But a self-focus distorts that God-given ambition and turns it toward having a little (or a lot) more money or a higher status, being better looking or being a little taller or a little shorter, having a better house or living in a better neighborhood, piling up a few more accolades and getting more compliments, and on and on. And all those things we think will make us content end up satisfying us for a moment—until we're discontent again and start reaching for more.

One definition of *contentment* is being happy enough with what you have or who you are, not desiring something more or different. In other words, it's being satisfied—not complacent, but not unhappy with where you are either. You realize what you have and who you are is good—not perfect, but enough to be fulfilled.

How content are you? In quiet moments when you have nothing to distract you, how unsettled do you feel? In all honesty, what do you believe would make you content? The clearer you get with that, the more powerfully God will speak to you in the following pages. If you're able to identify those longings—the things that make you think, *When I have that, I'll be happy. When I become that, I'll feel satisfied*—you'll recognize which ones will really bring contentment and which ones won't.

The problem with contentment, in purely human terms—in our natural, self-focused ambitions—is that the horizon is always moving. You can probably remember a time when you really wanted something and actually ended up getting it. When you're just learning to drive, you think you'd be content with any kind of car, even an old, beat-up junker. But when you get it and it starts having problems, you begin to think of a better car that runs well. Then when you've got that one, you want one that runs well and looks nice. Then you want one that runs well, looks nice, and sends a certain message about where you are in life. It's human nature; we all tend to think that way with cars, houses, degrees, jobs, even relationships. The goal just keeps moving, perhaps to something better, or maybe even just to anything else, as long as it's different.

Two drastic extremes have emerged as people have tried to solve this problem of contentment throughout the ages. One response has been to get more—to keep acquiring, conquering, achieving, expanding, and never stopping until you run out of objectives. The Roman Empire is a good example of that thirst for conquest. There's always a little bit more to acquire, a few more territories to conquer, a lot more wealth and power to be gained.

That didn't work for the Empire—one of the biggest reasons for its downfall was the difficulty in governing such a vast territory—and we know from experience it doesn't work for us personally either. Sure, it's nice to have things, and there's something very satisfying about climbing the ladder or accumulating a bit more. But you've probably noticed how your desires keep changing—how last year's phone that made you so happy then doesn't have all the best features now, or those stylish clothes don't make you feel quite as trendy a few months later. There's no end to that process. J. Paul Getty was once asked what it takes to really be satisfied. His answer was, "Just a little bit more." He recognized the futility. Contentment and the peace we seek never quite come.

The other extreme approach to this problem of contentment is detachment. If you don't care about anything, then you're always content with what you have. This is a prominent theme in some Eastern religions, some streams of Western philosophy, and certain periods and branches of Christian thought. A Stoic philosopher recommended envisioning your clay pots breaking as practice for experiencing the death of your loved ones because both are inevitable; close attachments lead to greater discontentment when they are lost. Stoics believed virtue mattered above all else, and everything else was valuable only insofar as it aided the practice of virtue. This line of reasoning encourages releasing things, acquiring less, and even giving up what you have in order to have peace. It also quenches love because love involves too much emotion. As scholar and historian T. R. Glover suggested, the Stoics made the heart a desert and called it peace.[1]

In extreme forms, this approach to contentment is called "asceticism." It majors on self-denial, but it never quite succeeds in creating peace or contentment. Human beings were designed for more than the bare essentials, materially and relationally, and even though it's good to know how to get by in times of hardship—we'll see Paul's statement on that soon—deprivation and detachment don't lead to peace. In fact, they usually lead to even greater anxiety.

How Can Our Souls Be Satisfied?

If getting more and more doesn't give us contentment, and if desiring less and less doesn't bring it either, we have a bit of a problem. How can we experience the peace we long for?

Paul, inspired by the Holy Spirit, gives us an answer in Philippians 4. Empowered by God's Spirit, we can actually live our lives in such a way that whether we feel like we're on a mountaintop or in a deep valley, we can say, "It is well with my soul." As with virtually everything in the Christian life, this is a journey, not an instant fix. But it's profound and desperately needed in a world that is constantly on a search for happiness.

Remember, when Paul writes, he is in confinement and awaiting trial to determine if he will live or die. He has been through several difficult years, and really a difficult life since becoming a Christian. He has scars and probably some broken bones that have never fully healed and is living under house arrest or in a Roman prison cell. But he has a good relationship with the Philippian church, and apart from instructions about the relational conflict there, his letter is mostly filled with words of joy and celebration of God's goodness.

During his confinement, the believers at Philippi sent one of their own to Paul with a monetary gift—a very useful favor, since Roman prisoners usually had to support themselves without any means of employment. One of the reasons for Paul's letter is to thank them for their generosity.

> I rejoiced greatly in the Lord that at last you renewed your concern for me. Indeed, you were concerned, but you had no opportunity to show it. I am not saying this because I am in need, for *I have learned to be content whatever the circumstances*. I know what it is to be in need, and I know what it is to have plenty. *I have learned the secret of being content in any and every situation*, whether well fed or hungry, whether living in plenty or in want. I can do all this through him who gives me strength. (Philippians 4:10–13, italics added)

Here Paul is essentially saying, "I know we had some great times together and saw God do some amazing things in birthing this church, but we've lost track of each other over the years. I've always known you cared, and I rejoice that you've taken this opportunity to show it." He says they have "renewed" their concern for him—the same word for a dormant flower now beginning to bloom. It's a beautiful picture, and Paul is actually happy in the midst of these difficult circumstances.

In fact, that's how this section of the letter begins: "I rejoiced greatly." And in order to assure them that this joy is genuine, he goes on to say that he is not actually in need but is at peace with whatever he has, whether a lot or a little. "I have learned the secret of being content in any and every situation," he tells them, "whether well fed or hungry, whether living in plenty or in want."

Twice in this short passage Paul says, "I have learned." This isn't present tense. It comes from past experience, and it's a skill Paul already has in his repertoire. On one hand, he has a brilliant mind, a great education, an upper-crust pedigree from a respected family, Roman citizenship, and at least in his early adulthood, a sterling reputation. He has had well-off friends like Barnabas and has known what the finer life is like. On the other hand, he has been beaten within a lash of his life on multiple occasions (and once left for dead), shipwrecked, betrayed by close friends who left the faith, imprisoned, insulted, scandalized, and plotted against. He has worn the scars and felt the hunger pangs to prove it. He knows hardship as well as anybody and more than most. And in all the ups and downs, the thread that connects all these experiences is a supernatural relationship with Jesus.

Clearly this is not theory or just a philosophy for Paul. If someone were to put this in modern terms, it's like saying, "I've had tons of money in the bank, gone to the finest restaurants, driven the best cars, and felt like everything was going my way. And I've also been broke, had close friends walk out on me, lost my health, lived with pain, and felt like everything is going against me. And through my relationship with Christ, I can honestly say at any of those moments, 'I'm fine.'" The last line of this passage (v. 13) is the key: "I can do all this through him who gives me strength."

For Paul, then, peace is not a thing to be achieved but a secret to be discovered. There's a way to find it apart from all the strategies of conquest and detachment the world has come up

Peace is not a thing to be achieved but a secret to be discovered.

with. It's possible to be truly at peace, not just faking it, in every situation in life, even when we aren't thrilled with what's going on. It isn't dependent on circumstances. You can actually be satisfied with who you are, where you are, what you have, and what you're doing as long as you're abiding in a deep relationship with Jesus.

This kind of contentment does not mean lying back on the couch and letting whatever is going to happen just happen. It isn't fatalism. You can still press ahead toward becoming everything you want to be in the process. Paul certainly did. It's a detachment from outward circumstances and anxieties, but not from inner purpose and personal relationships. Even in the midst of all the ups and downs of that turbulent journey, there's a supernatural peace in your heart.

But that raises an obvious question. How do ordinary people like you and me experience this kind of supernatural peace?

The Answer: Four Principles, Four Practices

Paul understood that contentment is a moving target. He knew from experience that gaining more and more would never be enough, and there were plenty of Stoics in his day to demonstrate that getting less and less—or becoming more and more detached—wasn't the answer either. So in this passage to the Philippians, where he calls contentment a "secret," he lays out four principles and practices we can follow to obtain it.

Keep in mind that these are doable principles and practices, not unreachable ideals. They are steps we can take to learn to be at peace 24/7, just as we learned to ride a bike or mastered a professional skill. We've touched on some of them, but we need to look at them in more depth. When we learn these, we are equipped for any situation we will ever encounter.

PRINCIPLE 1: Contentment is not dependent on our circumstances. Most of us have been taught unconsciously that there's a huge gap between our circumstances and our desires, and all we need to do is close that gap and we'll be happy. That's what the commercials tell us, right? We've been exposed to this message all our lives because it's the way the world thinks. I call it "the when-then syndrome": *When* you get married, get that job, have that house, drive that car, or whatever your particular desire is, *then* you'll be satisfied. Maybe you're waiting for your marriage to hit on all cylinders or your kids to grow up with good and healthy behaviors. It might be a certain career or a level of achievement within that career. It can be really big-ticket items or smaller steps along the way, like making a team or having enough money to remodel the kitchen. Large or small, the issue is always "when." And when "when" happens, "then" contentment and peace come.

The only way to get out of this never-ending cycle is to identify and break the lie.

As we've seen, this is a lie. Lots of people have gotten from the "when" to the "then" and are still very unhappy. Like cats chasing their tails, they keep increasing the speed of the chase but still never catch up. The only way to get out of this never-ending cycle is to identify and break the lie. How?

PRACTICE 1: **Be grateful.** Develop the discipline of thanking God for what you have rather than focusing on what you don't have. Gratitude is a very effective antidote to the never-ending chase. Billions of dollars are spent every year on advertising that is designed to make people discontent and put the possibility of contentment in front of them through a certain product or lifestyle—food, drink, clothing, jobs, cars, diets, surgery, grooming products, and on and on. Any of these can be enjoyed and might be nice to have. None of them have the power to make us content in themselves.

Paul interrupts this human tendency of focusing on what we don't have to say, "I have learned to be content whatever the circumstances." The rest of the letter backs that up. He rejoices and gives thanks throughout for all the great things that are happening. He even turns all the negative circumstances in chapter 1—his imprisonment, rivalrous preachers, and the possibility of his death—into positive situations that he is grateful for. Moment by moment, he has learned by practice to give thanks for what he does have, even in the midst of hardship.

Gratitude is not just a nice suggestion.

Gratitude is not just a nice suggestion. In three short verses in a letter to the Thessalonians, he makes it a command: "Rejoice always, pray continually, give thanks in all circumstances; for this is God's will for you in Christ Jesus" (1 Thessalonians 5:16–18). We are called to be thankful.

I've learned the hard way how a lack of gratitude can subtly but tragically turn us into very discontent people. I married a wonderful woman named Theresa without any premarital counseling or experience in what married life was supposed to be like. We both loved God, I was going to seminary, and that was supposed to be enough. That saying about "opposites attracting" was true for us. And at first, that was awesome. Our differences drew us together like magnets.

But several months into our marriage, those opposites became sticking points. What I once saw as "faithful" became "rigid." Where she once had integrity, now she was just picky. And my list of complaints was growing. Overall, I think we had a pretty good marriage. But my focus was on the 10 percent that was really rubbing me the wrong way. I thought that if she could just improve on five or six things, we would have a great marriage. When . . . then.

I helped Theresa embark on a self-help program designed just for her so she could be the wife she needed to be. She became my project. If we could just focus on those areas she needed to develop and change, things would get better. I didn't say any of this, of course. I wasn't that naïve. But it didn't make sense to me that we would drive each other crazy if we both loved God, loved each other, and were headed into the ministry. It's embarrassing to look back and see how arrogant I was about marriage and my own less-than-desirable traits that were producing conflict.

In the process of getting some wise pastoral counseling, however, which God graciously provided for us, I began the practice of being grateful and thanking God for the beauty and gifts and joys He had put into my wife. I quit focusing on the 10 percent that seemed, to me, to be lacking and celebrated the good that was there. It was a discipline at first—minds trained in "fix it" mode don't turn their attention away from the problems very easily—but over time, that discipline gave me a much more accurate perspective. I came to appreciate Theresa more and more, and it changed my world and our marriage.

I try to apply that same practice to every area of life. I still do it for my marriage; we still go through emotional challenges, and sometimes it helps to go to a coffee shop and start writing down, "She's so faithful, she prays for me, she's an amazing mother and grandmother, she's godly, she's kind and beautiful," and all the other wonderful qualities she has.

But this is just as effective with kids, jobs, lifestyles, and every other area of life. Most of us already have plenty of practice staring at the glass half-empty—or even the glass 2 percent empty—and need to be retrained to see what's there. When we do, our emotions change. We become less depressed and more content. Eventually we overflow with joy.

That's what Paul seemed to do not only in Philippians but in most of his letters. It profoundly changes our emotions and strips our discontentment of its foundation. The first and best thing we can do to grow in our experience of peace in difficult circumstances is to habitually practice being thankful.

PRINCIPLE 2: Contentment is an attitude we learn, not a thing we achieve. This secret to contentment dispels a very powerful myth: that contentment is a future event. Many of us seem to think there is a big breakthrough event waiting out there for us, something like a life lottery that takes us from just getting by to overabundance. That "lotto" can revolve around a person, an event, or a state of being, but it's still anchored in when-then thinking. And whenever it comes, we'll be happy.

In Philippians 4:11–12, Paul stresses that he has learned. Already. Our search for peace is not out there, external to us and waiting for us to get there. It is based on God doing something within us. It's internal and already available.

PRACTICE 2: Be teachable. If you really want to learn this skill of contentment as a way of life, add to your gratitude the art of being teachable. In whatever circumstances you face, ask God what He wants to teach you instead of telling Him what you want Him to change.

What would happen if a little mental recorder could track all your thoughts and play them back? What would your prayers sound like? For many of us, prayer requests focus on things we want God to give us, problems we want Him to solve, people we want Him to change, and situations we want Him to create or get us out of. We present Him with an agenda, as if His role is to be the genie who makes us happy, satisfied, and fulfilled.

> **Ask God what He wants to teach you instead of telling Him what you want Him to change.**

God does promise to provide for us, protect us, and answer our prayers. No question about that. But He isn't our genie, and His agenda is somewhat different from ours. He doesn't buy into the lie that if we only had this or that thing, person, or situation, we'd be content. Prayers focused almost exclusively on those things very often come from discontent people.

People who are at peace begin with, "Thank You, Lord." Even when things are difficult—and there's nothing wrong with telling Him we don't like certain situations—we choose to give thanks. And then content people add something to their gratitude: "Lord, teach me. What do You want me to learn in these circumstances? What are You trying to accomplish here, and how can I cooperate with that?" We learn to participate in His plans and leverage our situations rather than insist that something about them be changed.

I have a good friend who feels stuck. That's not an uncommon feeling. You have probably felt that way at some point in your life; that point may even be right now. Perhaps you've experienced the feeling of being stuck in your marriage, your job, your home life, or your school, and you know how frustrating it can be to keep trying to get unstuck without seeing breakthrough. That's where this friend is. He's tried everything, and he's really bummed out. He just can't make the right things happen.

We met one morning for coffee, and he pulled out a pen and started diagramming on a napkin. "God spoke to me," he said. "I realized all the things I couldn't change, even though I had done all I could to change them." So he wrote down his life categories: God, family, himself.

"I always say it's God first, then my family, then me," he said. "Then I did a little profit-and-loss evaluation, an inventory of where I am and how I'm stuck. I keep hitting things that don't move, so I started wondering if God wanted to teach me something. And I asked."

He went on to describe his thought processes in conversation with God, and what he thought God was teaching him about his relationship with God, his family, and himself. He looked at all his activities and where his energy was going, and even though he mentally placed God first, most of what he was doing was directed toward himself. He realized his words—his commitment to place God first and his family next, above himself—didn't really line up with his actions. So he reorganized his life, reprioritized, moved some things around, and said, "Okay, I want to learn."

That changed things. He realized what we all eventually discover for ourselves: that the goal of life is not self-actualization. It's not to be fulfilled and have everything go our way. God's primary agenda in your life is to make you like His Son, to use all the ups and downs in a fallen world to develop that vital relationship with Jesus by the power of His Spirit, rooted in His Word, in the context of authentic community, so that little by little you begin to think, talk, and serve like Jesus. It's for moms, dads, children, siblings, coworkers, and neighbors to embody the nature of God in Christ.

God's primary agenda in your life is to make you like His Son.

If you've struggled with that same discrepancy between your stated priorities and your actual investments of time, energy, emotions, and resources, this is where it's leading. When that vital relationship with Jesus becomes your priority, there will be people in your life who don't understand how you can go through the hard times or the injustice you're facing, who wonder how you keep such a level head in the midst of successes and abundance, who can't believe you aren't undone by the financial crisis or the pandemic that everyone is so worried about, who see the same version of you no matter what you're going through. You may still experience and express a range of emotions through those ups and downs, and you may need to work through some of them with God, but you begin to take on His nature and His peace. You manifest a supernatural calm and confidence regardless of your circumstances. You seem a lot more like Jesus than the disciples in that storm-tossed boat.

That's God's agenda for you, and when you become teachable in the midst of your circumstances, you learn what you can change and stop focusing on things you can't change. In any situation, you are able to thank God for what you do have and quit dwelling on what you don't have. And you begin to see every circumstance as an opportunity to demonstrate something of the nature of God and see it being formed in you.

PRINCIPLE 3: Prosperity does not have the power to give us peace and contentment, nor poverty the power to take it away. The secret of contentment challenges our modern assumption that more is better. This assumption is an American ideal and a common belief in today's global economy. But if inner peace is not based on circumstances and is an attitude we can learn, it can't be tied to our prosperity or lack.

Paul demonstrates the point himself in verse 12: "I know what it is to be in need, and I know what it is to have plenty." He's had a lot, and he's had nothing, and neither situation has defined his level of contentment. His word for "plenty" was also commonly used for fattened livestock. In other words, he is saying he has lived in the lap of luxury and knows it can't deliver happiness. But he has also experienced extreme hardship, including being hungry, thirsty, cold, and naked. (He provides a longer list of examples in 2 Corinthians 11:24–28.) None of those situations, whether positive or negative, have changed his level of peace and contentment.

You may have experienced extremes too. I know I have. In many respects, I've been very blessed and fortunate to live in a rich society with access to good medical care and many luxuries not available in some parts of the world. But I've also been in situations where I didn't know if I was going to come out alive. I've heard biopsy reports that confirmed cancer in loved ones. I've wondered how I was going to make it without this person in my life or how family and friends were going to get by without me if something happened to me. I have to agree with Paul: those kinds of situations can't take peace away from me, and the opposite situations will never be able to give it to me. It has to come from something beyond our circumstances.

PRACTICE 3: Be flexible. We begin by being grateful and then by being teachable. But what happens when God shows you something you didn't necessarily want to learn? Being flexible means you are open to change—in your own life and in the world around you. It's not just asking God what He wants you to learn; it's asking how He wants you to change in light of what you're learning.

When my friend sat down at the table and showed me his list of priorities, he put it all in context. "I've got a huge presentation to make for this big corporation, and there's a lot riding on it. I normally obsess over these things and over-prepare for them, working through every detail and trying to make sure nothing is left to chance. My career feels like a high-stakes project, and I've always chosen to prioritize it. But my wife wanted to get away and have some fun. And since God had just showed me where I was mixing up my priorities . . . well, I did it." And he described how he got up really early in the morning to put in about two hours of work on the presentation, and said, "Lord, I really need You to show up." Then he leaned in and said, "What's amazing is that the presentation went better than it would have if I had spent the whole day on it."

He was flexible. He took what God had told him and applied it to a real-life situation, even though it went against his grain and required a huge shift in thinking. When God says, "Here's how I want you to be more like My Son," what's the next step? It isn't the status quo. You have to break the lie that prosperity is going to get you where you need to go.

I'm one of those weird people who is going to bed about the time everyone else is getting revved up to have a great evening. Then while everyone else is sleeping, I'm usually up working. It's just how God made me. But it isn't easy finding a good place to work in the wee hours of the morning.

I found a little coffee shop that bakes donuts and bagels all night long and serves the kind of coffee I like. I'd go in there to spend some time with God and begin my workday, and I got to know people who seem to share the same weird schedule. One of the regulars was a young man I got to know pretty well. He came to California, began coming to our church, and eventually got pretty involved, and went to work at a Christian camp at minimum wage.

One morning as we shared coffee and a bagel, I asked him about his spiritual journey. I was captivated as his story unfolded and said, "That would make a great book."

"That's why I come in here so early," he said. "I'm revising the first edition for a publisher. Would you like to read it?"

He handed me a copy of *True Riches*, and I read the back cover.[2] At twenty-three, he had a degree in finance and plenty of credentials. He told the story of having three credit cards and borrowing as much cash as he could on each one, working his way onto the trading floor in Chicago, and going from dead broke to being a multimillionaire at twenty-five, with everything the world has to offer in his lap. Then at twenty-eight he was broke again, and again earned it all back the next year.

"God wanted to teach me something," he said. "I could get anything in the world I wanted. Do you know how scary it is to say you know Christ alone can deliver but unconsciously believe otherwise? I went into a deep depression. So I came here to serve people at minimum wage because I wanted to learn to be content. I want peace that doesn't ride the waves of circumstances I can't control."

How many people know Christ, believe the Holy Spirit lives in their hearts and lives, claim the Bible as truth, and behind the curtain of their soul still believe they have to get a good enough SAT score, make that team, climb the corporate ladder, land at the right firm, find that perfect spouse, or move into the right neighborhood to find peace? We unconsciously buy into that lie that prosperity can deliver, even when our words deny it. Paul's words sound like radical Christianity to many believers.

The flip side of that truth is that poverty has no power to take away our peace. Just as prosperity can't deliver it, lack can't destroy it. Paul said he was content even in those times when he had nothing.

I'll never forget a time in the Philippines when I was on a basketball team that traveled throughout the islands to play local teams and share Christ with the community. A young Filipino who traveled with us desperately wanted to show me his home. "You've got to come see it," he said.

"Sure," I said, and we got on his motorcycle to weave in and out of Manila traffic—no rules, as far as I could tell—to get to where he lived. We were weaving in and out of "lanes," dodging cars and trucks and all sorts of other vehicles. I was starting to wonder what I had gotten into. I was praying the whole way that I'd get to see Theresa and the kids again.

A missionary friend warned me that the young man lived in the slums, but I had no idea exactly what that meant until we got there. It was like nothing I had experienced. There was a hill with cardboard shacks against each other as far as the eye could see. In one area, there were a few wooden crates—that was the upper-middle class, I think—and then a few "elite" shacks with tin roofs to help for the rain. Thousands upon thousands of people, with no evidence of plumbing in sight.

Somehow this passionate young man had figured out how to extend a wire a long way from the one light pole and through his roof, so he attached a light bulb and opened up his home at night to read Scripture for anyone who wanted to hear. He was proud to be the only one in his area with a light.

We walked through a maze of people to get to his nine-by-six room. He had dug out a smaller area where he cooked. He introduced me to his wife and sons and said, "Chip, I'm so glad you would come to my home." You'd think he owned the Taj Majal.

"Where do you sleep?" I asked.

He looked at me like I was crazy. "Right here." He pointed to a small cot. "I curl my body this way, my wife curls that way, and we put our boys in the middle." Then he pointed to where he cooked, as if to emphasize that he had a two-level house. He had a light bulb, a dug-out level, a large enough bed for four, and was grateful for how good God had been to him. The most striking thing about him was the smile that radiated from his face and the joy in his heart.

Poverty doesn't have the power to rob our peace.

Poverty doesn't have the power to rob our peace. Paul says you can learn to be content in any situation. Sure, you will always be able to improve your golf swing, update your home, or get a better position. Go for it. But don't hang your contentment on those things. If you will practice being *grateful*, become *teachable*, and are *flexible* in every situation, you will be very close to having the heart and soul of someone who might as well have a million dollars in the bank and fulfilling relationships all in order, wondering how life could get better.

PRINCIPLE 4: Only Christ has the power to give us a peace that transcends all life's variables. Even believers buy into the lie that contentment can be found apart from God. But the testimony of those who get what they wanted and realize how much they need Him is that it can't. We can't blame unbelievers for thinking that the right situations, possessions, relationships, accomplishments, and status will do it for them because that's all they know to envision. In fact, that's how many of them become believers—they reach their goals and realize there's still something missing. But no one reaches contentment and experiences peace that transcends life's variables without connecting to the God above them.

Everyone seems to have a conscious or unconscious box full of treasures that they keep striving to reach. It's like a pot at the end of the rainbow. It keeps people walking, working, running on the treadmill that never ends. Sometimes they even reach their dreams and step into that little picture they drew for themselves. But instead of sitting around the table celebrating all the time, instead of being satisfied with what they've achieved, they're still restless. The picture doesn't look quite as good in the hand as it did on the horizon. That box turns out to be surprisingly empty.

In 2015, I had the privilege of leading chapel for the Seattle Seahawks when they came to San Francisco to play the 49ers. It was the year after they had beat the Broncos to win the Super Bowl. As the players in the room discussed what I shared from the Scriptures, a theme emerged. They all talked about the "letdown." Not that it wasn't wonderful to be world champions and accomplish such a challenging goal, but over and over I heard, "I thought it would feel different"—that reaching the top would be a lot "bigger" or more satisfying. The dream of every athlete is to be the world champion in their sport, but even when you arrive, it doesn't have the power to bring lasting peace.

The reason so many people come to Christ after they have given all the time, energy, and focus to a goal that turned out to be unfulfilling is that they have finally realized their need. It's the same reason people come to Christ out of extraordinary pain. Success and pain can both lead to hunger and thirst for a Savior because the world system can't give us what we need.

Believers arrive at that same realization when we think our peace comes from Jesus *plus* a great family, a good job, or a healthy body. The "plus" always gets us in trouble. We essentially tell God that when He delivers the "plus" and adds it to Jesus, we'll be happy and fulfilled. That's a spiritual version of the same journey unbelievers go on, but that's not the way life works. It's still a lie. We may not end up as empty as those without Christ, but it can feel that way if we've placed our hopes in Him plus something else.

Many Christians have lost their peace and wonder why.

The energy, skills, talents, time, money, and other resources God gives us to do something great with our lives for the sake of His kingdom can be subtly, destructively turned inward. We end up chasing something that doesn't exist, and we come up empty. That's why one of the fastest growing professions among believers in the last few decades has been Christian counseling. I'm grateful for counselors—I've benefited from them myself—but one of the reasons they are so needed is that believers have bought into the never-ending chase for contentment. Many Christians have lost their peace and wonder why.

PRACTICE 4: Be confident. If only Christ can give you the peace that transcends all circumstances—if that's the final secret of success added to being *grateful*, *teachable*, and *flexible*—then that's where we turn for strength. Maybe you've tried to change before and no longer think you can. If so, Philippians 4:13 is the key: "I can do all this through him who gives me strength."

Moment by moment, relationship by relationship, decision by decision, through every disappointment, you can have confidence that you can fulfill everything God wants you to do. It doesn't come by lying on the couch and thinking you might try that someday. The confidence comes by faith.

By faith, you begin by thanking God for whatever you do have. Then you commit to being teachable and learning how God wants to direct you. You become flexible enough to embrace change, reorienting your life around what matters, putting God and others first, even when there's a cost or it goes against your deeply ingrained ways.

Is it hard? Of course. Is it possible? Absolutely. But here's the key: When you receive the power of His Word, energized by His Spirit, in the context of genuine, loving community relationships, God will give you whatever you need to have a quiet heart that is completely at peace. Through the fellowship of His Son and the power of His Spirit, you can respond with all the courage and faith you need to be content and have peace in any situation in life. You can do all things through the One who strengthens you.

I recently received a letter from someone who wanted to thank me for some teachings that had been helpful to him.

But after that, seemingly out of the blue, he added some comments that get right to the heart of this issue of contentment. I'll paraphrase his story, but it went something like this:

> It seems like I keep running into people who think that if they can only perform at a high enough level, if they can only get enough applause or admiration, their life will have meaning. In the past year, I've spoken to so many in these situations, and I've seen it in my own life. But that doesn't do it.
>
> People put everything into being on the cheerleading squad, working their way to the top of the corporate ladder, making the dean's list, wearing a Super Bowl ring, or becoming a major political player. They spend every ounce of time and energy on these earthly goals, convinced that when they achieve them, they will finally have the self-esteem and confidence and peace they desperately want.
>
> But it seems to me, when they reach the pinnacle of what they thought would be successful, the sense of self-worth and contentment they long for is conspicuously absent. And the reason, I think, is that their goals were centered on what other people think rather than on what God thinks.
>
> I remember a sportswriter named Gary Smith once interviewed boxing legend Muhammad Ali at the fighter's farmhouse. Ali took Smith on a tour of his estate and led him into the barn, and the writer saw all of Ali's trophies, ribbons, and awards on the shelf, collecting dust, some of them even spattered with pigeon droppings—Golden Gloves, Olympic gold, World Champion. As they surveyed all the boxing memorabilia getting ruined, Muhammad

Ali said something very quietly to Smith. With his lips barely moving, he said, "I had the world, and it wasn't nothin'. Look now."[3]

What do you have now? What are you aiming for? What would it look like for you to be grateful, to be teachable, to be flexible, and to be confident God could give you whatever you need so that, as you grow in your contentment and experience His peace, circumstances would no longer have the power to touch you?

Here's the bottom line: Contentment is not a passive acceptance of the status quo. It's the positive assurance that God has supplied your needs and the release from unnecessary desires. Will you still have desires? Of course. You don't need to detach from everything in order to be content. And you certainly don't need to go to the other extreme and try to get all you can as if your contentment depended on it.

> **You are called to peace, and you already have everything you need to enter into it.**

No, you are called to peace, and you already have everything you need to enter into it. You have enough faith, courage, and supernatural empowerment to apply Paul's four keys and grow in peace daily. The *shalom* of God, which transcends every circumstance you will ever face, will guard your heart and mind, and God Himself will be with you.

QUESTIONS FOR DISCUSSION AND REFLECTION

1. Why is it so difficult to be genuinely content? What factors in our world make this so? What factors in our hearts make this so?

2. Why are both historical positions toward contentment doomed to failure?

3. How do each of the principles and practices relate to your present circumstances and attitudes about personal peace?

4. What action step will you take to reflect obedience to God's provision for your personal peace?

5. If you are going through this study in a group, take time to pray for one another. Ask God to help each member embrace His game plan for a life of personal peace. If you are going through this as personal study, spend some time praying the same for yourself.

CHAPTER 5

Choose Peace
in a Materialistic Culture

E ven if you've never heard of a "scouting report," you've probably done one.

In sports, your team puts together a scouting report by watching game film of another team and its players to figure out their strengths and weaknesses, where they can be exploited, where your strengths match up against their vulnerabilities, and what strategy to use when you play them.

In war, a small group of soldiers goes out in advance of a battle to scout out the adversary's positions and capabilities. One of my friends from years ago who had been a squad leader in Vietnam told me how he would frequently take about a dozen men out on a circular scouting mission, and sometimes after going through thick jungle they would find themselves at the edge of open areas of rice paddies, completely exposed. He'd send a couple scouts out from the natural cover, flat on their bellies, to check everything out and then motion to the rest if everything was okay. A good scouting report was a matter of life and death, and he saw people die in his arms because the report was wrong.

But we do a lighter version of this in everyday life, don't we? If a school friend wants your son or daughter to come over and spend the night, you make some phone calls, ask a few questions, check the internet for any sex offenders in the area, and make sure it's okay. It's not paranoid; you just have to be careful. Or when older students see a guy or girl they might be interested in, they ask so-and-so to ask so-and-so for some details to see if he or she might be worth pursuing. If you're interested in a job opening, you probably do a little research on the employer and check in with friends who might know others who work there to make sure it's actually a good opportunity. We conduct our own little scouting reports all the time.

In this chapter, we're going to look at contentment's greatest competitor and discover some ways to beat it. We'll continue in Philippians 4 to find out how to have peace in a materialistic culture. But first, let's look at another of Paul's passages that is essentially a scouting report about our battle. This report is even more serious than the scouting missions my friend had to do in Vietnam. People could lose their lives if the reports from him or his men were wrong, but people can lose their souls for eternity if they don't understand our enemy's tactics and their own vulnerabilities. Paul is dealing with an extremely serious issue.

A good scouting report does four basic things:

1. It identifies the foe.
2. It tells us how formidable the foe is.
3. It describes the foe's tactics.
4. It identifies where we are vulnerable.

So when false teachers were gaining influence in the first-century church, Paul wrote to Timothy to warn him about what was happening.

> They have an unhealthy interest in controversies and quarrels about words that result in . . . constant friction between people of corrupt mind, who have been robbed of the truth and who think that godliness is a means to financial gain.
>
> But godliness with contentment is great gain. For we brought nothing into the world, and we can take nothing out of it. But if we have food and clothing, we will be content with that. Those who want to get rich fall into temptation and a trap and into many foolish and harmful desires that plunge people into ruin and destruction. For the love of money is a root of all kinds of evil. Some people, eager for money, have wandered from the faith and pierced themselves with many griefs. (1 Timothy 6:4–10)

A teaching going around suggested that everything will turn out great for those who love God. Paul was pointing out the absurdity of the idea that walking with God and loving Jesus is a way to get rich. Sounds pretty familiar, doesn't it? That idea is still around. But people who believe such things, according to Scripture, "have been robbed of the truth."

People can lose their souls for eternity if they don't understand our enemy's tactics.

By contrast, Paul argues, "Godliness with contentment is great gain." What we get from walking with God, serving Him, and loving Him is a sense of supernatural sufficiency and peace in Christ. And then He follows this up with two facts that explain why this is true: (1) we brought nothing into the world and can take nothing out of it; and (2) if we have food and clothing, that's enough for us to be content.

In other words, Paul says, these teachers are making false promises, and people are wasting their lives on them. We come into the world as naked babies, and people may put nice clothes on us and give us a lot of wonderful things, but when we die, it doesn't matter if they put us in an expensive, gilded casket or a simple wooden box. A hundred percent of human beings come in with nothing and leave with nothing. And if, in the meantime, we have food and clothing—literally, a "covering"—to keep us nourished and protected from the elements, we really have all we need.

Then comes the scouting report: "Those who want to get rich fall into temptation and a trap and into many foolish and harmful desires that plunge people into ruin and destruction" (v. 9). Where does the ruin and destruction come from? "The love of money is a root of all kinds of evil. Some people, eager for money, have wandered from the faith and pierced themselves with many griefs" (v. 10). Paul is bothered that this is happening and wants to make sure Timothy stewards his leadership well and steers people away from the dangers of this temptation. Whether rich or poor, it is extremely risky for people to crave something that could cause them to drift away from their faith.

The Scouting Report's Four Questions

If a good scouting report addresses four key questions—who the foe is, how formidable the foe is, what the foe's tactics are, and where our vulnerabilities are—we should expect to find answers to each of these in Paul's words to Timothy.

Who is our foe? The technical name for the adversary Paul identifies is *philarguria*. It's the word translated as "love of money"—greed, or what we would today call *materialism*, that belief we examined in the last chapter that we just need more, more, and more to be happy. That's the foe Paul was dealing with and that we continue to deal with today.

How formidable is our foe? Paul is not reserved in his vocabulary when describing the dangers of avarice. Certain words serve as cues that we are dealing with a very formidable foe: *plunge, ruin, destruction, all kinds of evil, wandered, pierced, griefs*. The love of money is not primarily a financial problem. It's a heart issue. It skews our priorities and damages our relationships. About 60 percent of failed marriages can trace the failure back to disagreements about finances.

This is a powerful, deadly, ruthless enemy that can distort and destroy our spiritual, physical, emotional, and relational life. It can affect our eternal destiny.

The love of money is not primarily a financial problem. It's a heart issue.

What are the foe's tactics? Notice the words *temptation*, *trap*, *foolish*, and *harmful desires*, and a clear strategy begins to emerge. Temptation is almost always the prompt or urge to get something good in a bad way. It's missing the mark, a trap or a lure, that shiny thing a fish sees before it bites into a hook. Money is like that. It promises power, position, popularity, possessions, and a lifestyle that we think will make life easier and better. But when we start chasing it, the hook catches us and draws us in directions we didn't necessarily want to go.

The pursuit of money can destroy relationships and alienate us from God, both of which are far too high a price to pay for what we get in return. Jesus said the worries of the world and the deceitfulness of riches keep the Word of God from growing in us (Matthew 13:22). Little by little, our lives are strangled, and we end up with emptiness.

No one starts pursuing money with the intention of wandering from the faith. It isn't a willful decision. It just happens. We don't consciously think, *I love God, want Him to use my life for His purposes, and long for a good marriage and a fruitful career, but I think I'll just throw that all away and chase money instead*. It doesn't work that way. That's why Jesus called it the "deceitfulness of wealth" (Matthew 13:22). We don't realize what is happening while it is happening. So, as Paul puts it, we wander from the faith. We drift away like someone in a boat so engrossed in what's going on around him that the current takes him downstream, past the dock, and on to who knows where.

That's what this word *wander* means (1 Timothy 6:10). You wake up one day and you're far from Christ. Your priorities are out of order, your marriage is tense, you are consumed with your work, debt begins to grow, your kids are seeing the worst side of you, and everyone picks up on the fact that your life is oriented around having more. The result? You're pierced with grief. That's a powerful tactic.

Where are we vulnerable? Remember, this is a heart issue. And the heart can be deceitful above all else (Jeremiah 17:9). As believers, we've been given a new heart (Jeremiah 31:31–34), but we still have the potential to step outside that new creation and act in old ways. For most of us, the issue is not whether we are being deceived or are greedy. The question is how greedy we are. We are vulnerable in our hearts because we live in a culture that is constantly saturating us with messages of materialism and greed. We are bombarded with advertisements that are designed for the sole purpose of creating discontentment and then offering a false solution. Our old shoes, heels, hemlines, tapered cuts, cars, perfumes, jewelry, hairstyles, home furnishings, colors, patterns, and more are not good enough. We must need something new. To some degree or another, we have all been hooked.

> To some degree or another, we have all been hooked.

What are you going to do about that? The answer isn't necessarily to run in the other direction and avoid buying anything ever again. But if the consequences of the love of money are ruin, destruction, and grief, it demands that we each check our own hearts—frequently.

Jesus talked about money a lot, usually in a warning. He didn't say money was bad, necessarily; His ministry received donations (Luke 8:1–3). But He knew the dangers of serving money instead of God (Luke 16:13)—of turning our worship away from God and toward "mammon" and letting greed and materialism drive our lives. He understood where we were vulnerable.

We know from the context of Scripture as a whole that having money is not bad in itself, but it is dangerous. As we will see, Paul will go on in his instructions to Timothy to say, "Command those who are rich in this present world not to be arrogant nor to put their hope in wealth, which is so uncertain, but to put their hope in God, who richly provides us with everything for our enjoyment" (1 Timothy 6:17). He doesn't tell those who are rich in this present world not to be rich. He tells them where to invest their hearts. The desire for money can be a road to destruction or a great kingdom asset. But vulnerable, tempted hearts so often turn it to the former rather than the latter. As Paul continues his letter to the Philippians, we will see how he views money as a vehicle of true worship rather than as a means of materialistic gain. He shows us how to overcome this formidable foe of materialism and experience true peace.

Breaking the Grip of Greed: Three Principles, Three Practices

By God's grace, through the power of His Spirit and His Word, we really can break the grip of greed. We saw in Paul's instructions to the Philippians in the last chapter how to learn contentment: through being grateful, teachable, flexible, and confident in the power of Christ at work in us (Philippians 4:10–13). That's a priceless lesson. In the next few verses, Paul and the Philippian church model what this antidote to greed looks like in real life. From their example, we can see three principles and three corresponding practices that will strip greed of its power in our hearts and minds.

PRINCIPLE 1: **Develop personal compassion.** Greed hardens your heart. It turns your focus to money, which often translates into things and experiences, which often take a higher place in our lives than God and people. The only way to reverse that trend is to have our hearts tenderized, to soften them toward God and people. In other words, we must intentionally develop compassion.

PRACTICE 1: **Put others' needs ahead of your wants.** Developing compassion is the "what." This is the "how." Identify some of your wants, find someone with a real need, and then decide to let go of your want to meet their need. This will require time, energy, or money that you would have spent on yourself to be redirected to someone else. That's an act of compassion, and as you learn to do it eagerly rather than grudgingly, it undoes the power of greed in your heart.

133

Paul identifies this kind of compassion in the Philippian believers. Immediately after he says he can do all things through Christ, who gives him strength, he highlights their generosity: "It was good of you to share in my troubles" (Philippians 4:14). As far as we can tell, piecing together the origins of the Philippian church in Acts 16 and comments Paul makes in his letters, this church began about ten years earlier. The church was birthed in turmoil; it's where Paul and Silas were beaten and imprisoned overnight for starting a riot, when all they had done was to cast an evil spirit out of a slave girl. They worshiped in jail, an earthquake broke their chains and opened the doors, they shared the gospel with the jailer, and the believers meeting in Lydia's home began to multiply. But Paul left town after those turbulent events and developed a close bond with this church in the following years.

Here he recalls those early years, when the Philippian believers were supporting his ministry. "It was good of you," he tells them—it was beautiful, winsome, an act of true fellowship when they shared with him. When? In his "troubles," a technical word used in the New Testament for the pain and suffering that comes from sharing Christ.

Then Paul continues reminiscing about the old days: "Moreover, as you Philippians know, in the early days of your acquaintance with the gospel, when I set out from Macedonia, not one church shared with me in the matter of giving and receiving, except you only" (Philippians 4:15). At first, this was the only church in the region to partner with him in a giving-and-receiving relationship. He is essentially reminding them how they had put his needs ahead of their wants and thanking them for doing the same thing again in this new situation of need.

This idea of giving and receiving is threaded throughout the New Testament. Those who receive spiritual food supply financial provision to those who give it so the ministry can go forward. Paul makes the point often in his letters, and it's a huge reason the church advanced in the first century. Early believers developed compassion in contrast to the greed of their culture.

As a pastor for more than three and a half decades, I've rarely met sincere followers of Jesus who don't want to be more compassionate and meet the needs of those less fortunate. Unfortunately, there's a very subtle lie, a mindset that prevents them from living that out. It goes something like this: *Someday, when I am earning a lot more money and have extra income, I'm going to really help others and invest in churches and ministries that accomplish these God-ordained purposes.* They honestly believe that they need to get more in order to give.

I've discovered that almost everybody sees him- or herself as middle class. Those who make less than average still see themselves as better off than many; those who make millions think of the billionaires, not themselves, as the rich ones who are better off. And in most cases, people sincerely think they need more in order to be more compassionate.

But that's not how compassion works. In one of his letters to the Corinthians, Paul wrote about the churches in Macedonia, which included Philippi, and how they gave generously, "even beyond their ability" (2 Corinthians 8:3) in a time of extreme poverty. In fact, they begged for the opportunity to contribute to people in need (2 Corinthians 8:1–5). That's a mark of compassion. It isn't dependent on supply. Compassionate people give regardless of their financial status.

When I first learned this principle, I was poor. Theresa and I were making less than a thousand dollars a month, we had three kids, I was going to seminary full time, and a representative from a well-known ministry came to chapel to speak to us about poverty relief and education in places where kids were starving.

There were about a thousand students in chapel that day, and the speaker showed us a video of poor kids in severely impoverished places. *I really wish I could help them,* I thought, *but I can barely pay my rent!* At the end of the video, the guy got up and said, "You're probably wondering why I would come to a seminary to show you this. A lot of you are trying to work two jobs while being a full-time student, and you're barely making it. So why would I come here?"

Yes, I thought. *I'm wondering the same thing. Why would you come here?*

"Before I answer that question, let me ask you another question. How many of you take your family out for a fast-food meal a couple times a month, just as a little treat?"

Almost every hand went up. That was a huge treat for our family. Two kids' meals were shared among three kids, Theresa and I would split a burger, everybody would drink water—

about fifteen dollars for all of us. That was a deal. We always looked forward to it.

Then the speaker put up a slide of one of those kids. "Going to McDonald's twice a month is a want. Would you be willing to give up that want once a month in order to meet this child's need? Can you sacrifice fifteen dollars a month to feed, educate, and share God's Word with a child who would otherwise not be able to eat or go to school?"

I'll never forget walking home that day with a picture of a child living in poverty whom I had committed to help. That was more than three decades ago, and it softened my heart and started a journey of compassion that continues to this day. I never would have started that journey if I had waited to give until I was well-off, because most of us don't ever see ourselves as well-off. It has to start where you are.

What does a heart of compassion look like in your life? Where can you take some of your wants and translate them into meeting others' needs? It's possible to give without loving someone, but it isn't possible to love without giving. And when you give, your heart grows more tender and you cultivate your compassion. That's the first step in breaking the power of greed and experiencing the peace of Christ.

> **It's possible to give without loving someone, but it isn't possible to love without giving.**

PRINCIPLE 2: Develop a generous spirit. Money can not only harden our hearts, it can make us protective of what we have. In amassing more, we pay a lot of attention to guarding what we already have so that we aren't losing anything while we are gaining. I get to see this when I preach about giving. Bodies and expressions stiffen. Walls go up. Some people unconsciously cross their arms as if to say, "I don't want anyone trying to tamper with my finances."

PRACTICE 2: **Release the very thing that has the power to consume you.** Compassion is like a muscle. We need not only to make our hearts tender toward God and others but also to get them flowing outward. We need to develop a generous spirit. And Paul's words in Philippians tell us that we can develop a generous spirit by releasing the very thing that has the power to consume us.

"Even when I was in Thessalonica, you sent me aid more than once when I was in need" (Philippians 4:16). What does Paul mean by "even when I was in Thessalonica"? Thessalonica was a lot better off financially than Philippi, and the Thessalonian believers should have easily been able to support his ministry. But they didn't necessarily have the spiritual maturity to do so. The Philippians did. Again and again, they sent him aid, even when they were in need themselves. They were systematic about it.

Paul explicitly recommended a systematic plan to the Corinthians. "Now about the collection for the Lord's people: Do what I told the Galatian churches to do. On the first day of every week, each one of you should set aside a sum of money in keeping with your income, saving it up, so that when I come no collections will have to be made" (1 Corinthians 16:1–2). He encouraged them to release a portion of their income every single week in order to develop their generosity to God and people in need.

This is not another "ought" or "should" to make us feel guilty. The practice addresses a heart issue and works toward our advantage in growing us up spiritually and supporting the ministry of God's kingdom on earth. Paul isn't placing just one more obligation on us. He is showing us a way to freedom and peace.

To put this in perspective, think about the way we tip servers in restaurants. When the service is good, we usually leave 15 percent as a minimum, sometimes a little more, because that's the dining culture we've created. Servers get paid from gifts of gratitude for their service.

Why is it that most of us would never think of leaving less than 10 or 15 percent on a check for a restaurant server, yet less than 3 percent of American Christians give 10 percent of their income to God on a regular basis?[1] What has happened sociologically to make one seem standard and the other seem like a burdensome obligation? It certainly isn't because servers deserve more; they do great work, but they don't create the food. They just bring it. Our lives were created by God, and He sustains us with every breath and heartbeat. He sacrificed His Son for us, raised Him from the dead, covered our sin, put His Spirit within us, sealed us forever in our relationship with Him, gave us spiritual gifts, provides for us every day, and told us to remember that it all belongs to Him. Scripture gives us a tithe as a starting point for giving back to Him, yet more than 97 percent of American believers don't even attempt the starting point. Why?

If you wondered whether materialism and greed have a grip on your life, this might be an indicator. Are you more faithful to your waiter or waitress than you are to the God who created your food and bought your salvation? If so, and if you see a lot of inconsistencies in your giving, now is the time to break the power of *philarguria* over your life. Jesus said our hearts will be where our treasure is (Matthew 6:21). We generally invest in our loves and desires, and our loves and desires grow in the areas we've invested in. The only way to address this heart issue is to proactively do the things that will soften our heart and cultivate generosity. It is a step of faith that becomes a lifestyle with practice.

I'm still growing in this area too. I was standing in line to get coffee at an airport recently, and the lady in front of me ordered a mocha. For whatever reason, it took the barista behind the counter an extraordinary amount of time to fix it. Another customer waiting behind me gave up and left. I was just standing there nurturing a critical spirit, thinking, *Come on, buddy, this is getting ridiculous. And it's not where I usually get my coffee, so I bet it's not going to be nearly as good. I can't believe I'm waiting this long for a substandard coffee.* My impatience was rapidly decreasing my generosity and peace.

I finally got my coffee, and then I went over to the sugar-and-cream stand. The lid on the creamer was loose, so my attempt to put in just a little turned into a cup of mostly milk. I was afraid to pour any out because I didn't know if the barista would refill it. But I went over to him and said, "Hey, do you think I could get a little grace?"

"What do you mean?"

"Listen, I put way too much cream in. If I dump some out, could you pour some more coffee in so it'll turn the right color?"

"Sure, I could do that." And he added some more coffee and made it just right.

As he handed it back to me, I thought, *This is a good moment for me to change my attitude.* I reached in my pocket and handed him a dollar. "Here's an extra buck. I just want to tell you, it's great to be around people with such a good attitude."

His tense, stoic demeanor gave way to an ear-to-ear grin. "Thanks, man!"

"No, thank you. I really appreciate it." It was obvious he was new on the job and I wasn't the first impatient and frustrated customer of the day.

One dollar's worth of generosity changed two guys' attitudes—his and mine. He relaxed and felt encouraged, and my critical spirit was transformed into a pretty good feeling about being able to bless him.

Do you see what issue is at stake here? Greed and generosity are not just about money. They aren't even about whether the church is getting what it needs to continue its ministry. They are mindsets, lifestyles, perspectives on the world that affect our moment-by-moment interactions and our future, and ultimately determine our peace. If you want to beat greed, you need to develop personal compassion for people and a generous spirit that blesses them. And don't be surprised if your joy level goes up and your peace of mind multiplies.

PRINCIPLE 3: Develop an eternal perspective. If we really believe there's life after death, a heaven and a hell, and that certain good things await people in heaven who follow God's ways, it changes the way we live. We begin to live for eternity rather than only for the here and now.

PRACTICE 3: Understand the inseparable relationship between your money and authentic worship. This is addressed in a variety of ways throughout Scripture, but the bottom line is that our worship and money are inseparably connected. Most people tend to put them in two distinct categories—what happens in our hearts and at church is worship, and what happens in our bank accounts is an entirely different matter. But every financial decision we make ends up being a worship decision of some kind.

> Every financial decision we make ends up being a worship decision of some kind.

Unfortunately, many pastors and churches talk about money only in the context of needing some. And because of that, many congregation members have gotten the impression that they are seen merely as potential donors, and they become resistant to the dreaded financial appeals. But that's a distortion that I and many other pastors ought to apologize for. Jesus talked about money more than he talked about heaven and hell combined. Money shouldn't be a bad word in the church. It's actually a fundamental indicator of our worship.

When spiritual leaders talk about money, it should almost always be in the larger context of using it well, being grateful, aligning our families with God's values, protecting our marriages, teaching our kids, and honoring God with our worship. Yes, churches and ministries have budgets and need income, but that's not the point. The fundamental point and priority in discussing money is the heart of the believer. When money has the right place in the heart—as a means rather than an end, as an opportunity to give rather than an opportunity to get—the budget issues are usually fine. Above all else, money is a spiritual issue.

Paul turned his words in Philippians in exactly that direction. After writing in financial and business terms to describe the church's gifts to him, he suddenly shifts to spiritual terms:

> Not that I desire your gifts; what I desire is that more be credited to your account. I have received full payment and have more than enough. I am amply supplied, now that I have received from Epaphroditus the gifts you sent. They are a fragrant offering, an acceptable sacrifice, pleasing to God. (Philippians 4:17–18)

Notice the progression. He has said he can do all things through Christ who strengthens him. He has thanked them for their gifts, not only in his captivity in Rome but also way back in the earliest days of the church and in his ministry in Thessalonica. And now he wants to make sure they understand his motives—that he is not focused on receiving gifts and having his needs met. Instead, he is focused on the good the Philippians' generosity brings to their account.

That phrase, "credited to your account," is as financially oriented as it sounds—an accounting term about debits and credits. Paul is essentially saying that the Philippians' heavenly profit-and-loss statement is in great shape because of their generosity. He has "received full payment," a picture of having the receipt in his hand. He is "amply supplied," having accepted the gift they sent with Epaphroditus. Paul's financial standing is not the issue now. He is focused on something much more important: the "fragrant offering" and "acceptable sacrifice" of the Philippians' worship through giving, which is "pleasing to God." They gave money, and the gift is of enormous value in their spiritual account.

A literal translation of that passage could look something like this: "When you did that, it was like a burnt offering, a fragrant, sweet smell that went up into the nostrils of God. He looked at it not as money but as a sacrifice of worship to Him, and it brought great pleasure and joy to His heart."

Clearly the issue is bigger than money here. The Philippians' gift reflects an eternal perspective, and Paul is making sure they recognize the relationship between their money and their worship. Every time we make a financial decision, every time we spend our money on something, we are choosing not to spend it on other things. We are providing a picture of what's important to us. God wants us to use money to meet our needs, and He is certainly not opposed to satisfying many of our wants. With deep gratitude, being satisfied in those desires can reflect our worship too. But what are we prioritizing? What does the hierarchy in our hearts look like?

Where is God in that hierarchy? Where are other people's needs in relation to our own wants?

Those are heart issues, and they are represented by something as mundane as money. Put simply, my money goes to the people, places, and things that matter most to me. It's like an MRI of my soul, my values, and my true worship.

King David was once told to build an altar on the threshing floor of a man named Araunah. When David tried to buy the threshing floor, Araunah offered it freely to his king. But David insisted on paying for it, and his reason was profound: "I will not sacrifice to the LORD my God burnt offerings that cost me nothing" (2 Samuel 24:24). Gifts from the heart are not minimal offerings of things we'll never miss. They cost something. They are sacrifices. They are reflections of what we love.

As you think about that last sentence, what would your money say about whom and what you love? My purpose in asking is not to send you on a guilt trip but to help you take any blinders off and see that peace is impossible if your heart is held captive. Giving begins to open up your heart and bring you into a place of freedom.

That's how we overcome greed with an eternal perspective. When we give our time, energy, talents, and financial gifts as acts of worship, a spiritual transaction occurs. A "credit" is added to our spiritual account. We acknowledge that impressing people and accumulating and enjoying everything we can now is not the end of the line—that there's more at stake than what we can get and spend in the present. We adopt the long view and live generously because of it. We take the things of this world and turn them into something of eternal value, and greed loses its power in our lives.

Scouting Recommendations

A good scouting report doesn't just give you information about the enemy's and your own strengths and weaknesses. It makes some recommendations based on that information. So let's go back to that letter Paul wrote to Timothy, the scouting report we looked at earlier in this chapter, and see what his recommendations are. He gives them in the form of four specific commands that will start us on a lifelong journey of peace by beating the monster of greed.

Before we do, there are a couple of things I think you should know. I'm well aware that you may be feeling overwhelmed as you read this. You may be juxtaposing the antidote to greed—having compassion, giving generously, and seeing with an eternal perspective—with massive debts and real frustration with where you are financially. No matter how many pictures of starving children you see, you've got no margin to give. The hook isn't just in your mouth; it's deep down inside. Are you forever out of God's will, then? Of course not. You can get out of this through a process that begins today. We'll dive deeper into that in the next chapter.

The other thing you should know is that I used to be a skeptic about this kind of message. I mentioned earlier that I didn't grow up in the church, and I've run into a lot of bad teaching after becoming a Christian too. I know what it's like to read teaching like this and think, *This is just leading up to an appeal to give to his ministry,* or *That's the church for you—always trying to sustain itself by milking all it can out of gullible people.* Please be assured that I'm not asking you to give to any particular ministry, and if giving to a church is a problem right now, give to some charity that serves people at their point of need. I do believe God wants us to give a regular percentage to whichever church we are involved in, but the more important point right now is just learning to be generous. It's not a matter of anybody's bottom line; it's a matter of the heart.

The four commands in Paul's scouting recommendations are very clear and concise:

> Command those who are rich in this present world not to be arrogant nor to put their hope in wealth, which is so uncertain, but to put their hope in God, who richly provides us with everything for our enjoyment. Command them to do good, to be rich in good deeds, and to be generous and willing to share. In this way they will lay up treasure for themselves as a firm foundation for the coming age, so that they may take hold of the life that is truly life. (1 Timothy 6:17–19)

1. Put your hope in God. Here God is identified as the one who provides for our enjoyment. Yes, it is important to be sacrificial in our giving, but it's equally important to enjoy what God has given us. The word used here clearly conveys the physical pleasures of this life. Giving generously is not a call to live in asceticism and poverty but to richly enjoy all God's good gifts and to be extravagantly generous as well.

You can't enjoy things if you're always worried about making the payments, so make sure your hope and contentment are rooted in God above all else. Don't strive for things that promise to make you content. Be content. But then enjoy what He has provided.

2. Be rich in good deeds. Like the Philippians, do things in a way that adds to your spiritual account. Recognize where true wealth is. This is a call to personal involvement, not just financial gifts.

3. Be generous. Focus more on giving than on getting. That heart of compassion you have developed will serve as a great motivator for a generous lifestyle.

4. Be willing to share. Being generous and rich in good deeds means giving away your time, energy, money, and possessions. Consider all your assets—time, money, materials, skills, talents, wisdom, and more—as community property. You steward them, of course, and that means knowing how to measure them in ways that don't lead to burnout and exhaustion. But it also means sharing your finances and yourself with a bigger purpose in mind.

The last line of this passage is a great reminder of that larger purpose: "In this way they will lay up treasure for themselves as a firm foundation for the coming age, so that they may take hold of the life that is truly life." We do this because the way we live now not only has an impact on other lives but also affects the quality of our experience in eternity. In other words, this scouting report guarantees that we will win the game.

That's what it means to "take hold of life that is truly life." In this life, relationships work better, creditors don't call, and instead of feeling guilty about what God has provided, you can simply be grateful for it, appreciating every opportunity to enjoy His gifts and share them generously with others.

This scouting report guarantees that we will win the game.

That kind of life is not hanging on the next big thing or waiting for some fulfillment "out there." It's a life in which, whether in plenty or in want, you know you can do all things through Christ who strengthens you.

If you long for that kind of life, ask God now to show you the extent to which greed has infiltrated your heart. Sit quietly and let Him speak to you. Be completely honest with Him and yourself. Then ask Him to show you the first step out of it. Don't look at every problem or the whole mountain of debt, if you have one. Don't examine every area of your life just yet. Start with something specific that God shows you, and then go from there. Then ask Him for the "next step" toward a heart of compassion, a generous spirit, and an eternal perspective, and do what He says. Ask Him who might help you on this journey—a counselor, pastor, or financial planner. You will have begun an adventure that is far more fulfilling than anything money can buy.

QUESTIONS FOR DISCUSSION AND REFLECTION

1. In Paul's "scouting report," what is contentment's greatest competitor? What makes this adversary such a formidable foe?

2. The theme of the book of Philippians is joy. How does the Philippian model (4:14–18) produce joy and personal peace?

3. How has greed crept into your heart and mind? In what ways have you experienced the futility and emptiness of its promises?

4. What practical steps are you going to take to follow the Philippian model toward personal peace?

CHAPTER 6

Choose Peace
in Tests of Faith

We began this journey looking for peace in the midst of conflicts, anxieties, circumstances, and challenges of this world. This chapter doesn't end the journey, of course. My hope is that it becomes a launching point into a new way of life, the beginning of a discovery process that will lead you into a quality of life many Christians never get to experience.

But that will only happen if you get to the end and make a conscious decision to activate your faith in this area. The title of this book and its chapters have not urged you just to have peace. They have prompted you to *choose* peace. There's a reason for that. Your peace and contentment only come through commitments you have made to embrace the truths God has given us in Scripture and live them out.

Before we continue, let's review some of those truths we have discovered in the last few chapters. After giving us instructions on having peace in our relationships and overcoming our anxieties through prayer, Paul turned his attention to the issue of contentment, and we explored his scouting report about the enemy of greed and Jesus's warnings about the place of money in our lives. We saw several truths:

1. Contentment is learned (Philippians 4:10–13). There is a secret to contentment, and we can learn it as a skill that will apply to any situation in our lives, regardless of whether our circumstances appear good or bad. We can choose peace in every situation!

2. Greed must die before contentment can live (Philippians 4:14–18). The way we get greed to die is by developing personal compassion, cultivating a generous spirit, and adopting an eternal perspective. We develop compassion by giving up our wants to meet other people's needs; we cultivate generosity by releasing the very thing (money) that consumes us; and we develop an eternal perspective by realizing that our money and our worship are not two separate categories of life but are inextricably connected.

3. Our treasure both reveals and directs the affections of our hearts (Matthew 6:21). Wherever your time, energy, talents, skills, and money go, your heart will be there. It is connected to your treasure. Your treasure has the ability not only to reflect your heart but to direct it as well. At different times in my life, this has been a very effective way to sort out my priorities or work on a relationship. When I've sensed my heart was not where God or I wanted it, I've started putting my treasure—my time, money, or energy—into whatever area I've needed to address. Sometimes it was my wife or one of my kids; at other times, I've realized my heart was hard or insensitive to another person or group. It's amazing how God has changed my heart in those times. As I gave more of my time, energy, or money where I knew God wanted them, my heart followed my investment.

These steps of faith and obedience will dramatically increase the peace and contentment in our lives, and they are part of an ongoing process that will last the rest of our lives. But they are also contested because virtually every advance in God's kingdom faces challenges. We will go through tests, and we need to know what to do when we encounter them.

Truth be told, we never know where our heart and values really lie until they are tested. The coronavirus global pandemic was a wake-up call for many sincere Christians when it first hit in early 2020. In the wake of death and economic fallout, more than a few shared with me that when money or people were removed from their lives, they realized they had made them idols without even knowing it. Tests have a way of revealing our real priorities—and what we are actually counting on for peace.

The Problem—and the Solution

Peace is a wonderful thing. Intellectually, we all want contentment. But we've seen that the way to get peace and contentment can be very counterintuitive. We receive by giving.

And for many people, that presents a problem. If you're deeply in debt, sweating over a stack of bills, and facing upcoming expenses like tuition for your kids or income for your retirement years, you might despair over the idea of becoming more compassionate and generous. Who's going to take care of *you*? That's a really big question a lot of people in difficult situations are wrestling with. At some point in the last few chapters, you might have started thinking, *What about me?*

Paul addresses that question in Philippians 4:19: "My God will meet all your needs according to the riches of his glory in Christ Jesus." This is a personal God who meets *all* the needs of those who have learned to live generously and compassionately—even in their most trying times.

> **This is a personal God who meets *all* the needs of those who have learned to live generously and compassionately—even in their most trying times.**

The church at Philippi was a generous church. As a whole, it didn't have a lot of money, though some of its members like Lydia were probably doing okay. They loved Paul, heard what was happening with him, decided his needs were bigger than some of their wants, and gave financially out of their compassion. Paul tells them in this letter that they have modeled the path of love and contentment—the life that is really life. So he reassured them, as if to say, "Here's what I want you to know. When you're generous like that and your priorities are in order, you can know when you're afraid of the future that my God—not the universe, not the force, not invisible factors or principles, but this very personal God—will supply all your needs." What kind of needs? Paul doesn't say. *All* is a big word. It includes spiritual, emotional, relational, physical, and financial needs. And He will do it according to the glorious riches of Jesus.

That's the promise: God's provision. If we will trust Him and live out this radical compassion and generosity, Paul says, God will make sure we have what we need. He'll take care of us.

With every promise, there's a premise—a condition we have to fulfill in order to receive what God is offering. We can never earn His gracious gifts, or course, but He does require us to respond in certain ways to receive them.

That's why some people who have been believers a long time come to a verse like this and think, *Okay, maybe in principle. But I've tried this, and it doesn't work.* No Christian really says that out loud, but we think things like this, don't we? We've prayed, God hasn't provided the way we thought He would, and we're left with unpaid bills and confusion about what went wrong. If this is you, let me try to clear up the confusion.

First, I'd suggest that sometimes we get our needs and our wants confused. If you've got enough to eat, a roof over your head, and you're warm in the winter, that's really all you need. God is not necessarily promising that you'll own your own home, have a second car, wear fancy clothes, and rest securely in your retirement plan, though He often graciously provides those things anyway. After giving generously, we might find ourselves unable to pay for our accustomed life-style and wonder why God isn't living up to His promise.

I had that very experience in seminary. I was working full-time selling life insurance while going to school full-time, and my job was based entirely on commissions. I'd make about $900 a month, which even in 1980 wasn't much money for a family of five. But there were times when a client would not pass a physical exam, so I didn't get my commission. We got into some pretty tight situations trying to figure out how to pay for rent and food. We'd dig quarters out of the back seat, pleading with God and claiming Philippians 4:19. I could tell story after story of God providing for our needs at the last minute. A check from an NFL quarterback I had met while he was in high school paid for rent and groceries one month. Once when we had no money in the bank, a letter and check from a missionary in India came the day our bills were due. These kinds of things happened so often and in such amazing ways that I began to quit worrying about finances, even though I never knew exactly how God would provide.

I still remember a really big lesson God taught us about His provision. The husband of the lady next door in our apart-ment complex walked out on her. She had a newborn and an older boy about the same age as our twin boys. She and Theresa had become good friends, and early one morning while I was reading my Bible, Theresa came to me with a great concern and an outrageous thought: "Chip, she's going to get kicked out of her apartment. We need to pay her rent."

"Honey, surely you jest," I said semi-sarcastically. But I quickly realized she wasn't smiling. "Theresa, we'd only have $10 left in the bank if we did that."

"Chip, I believe God wants us to pay her rent."

As I prayed about it, the still, small voice of the Holy Spirit confirmed Theresa's prompting to me, but I still didn't think it was a good idea. So I did what most people do in that situation. I tried to talk myself out of it. I told myself that still, small voice must have just been my imagination because the Holy Spirit was surely more aware of our financial situation than that. But I've learned that when you get thoughts about helping someone at great cost to yourself in ways that would bring glory to God, it's probably not from you.

I finally gave in after about three days. I was reluctant, but I agreed to do it. And my heart really did go out to her. Wanting to help was not the problem. Having the means to do it seemed like a big one. But we took everything but $10 out of the bank and paid her rent.

About nine days later, our own rent was due. "Okay, Lord," I prayed. "Philippians 4:19. You're going to supply all my needs, right? My rent's due!"

No money came. I'd seen miraculous things happen for the last two years, but this time there was no provision. Our rent contract gave us a three-day grace period. Still, no money came the next day. Or the next. On the third day, we had to pay.

"Lord, it's Your reputation on the line. What are You doing? Philippians 4:19—does it work or not?" I was pretty upset.

"How can I trust You in the future if You don't come through after we've sacrificially given to help our neighbor in crisis?"

As I was half praying and half complaining, I walked into our little living room and saw our TV. It wasn't worth much, but I thought, *Is that a need or a want?* Then I saw the stereo system I'd had for a few years. It was pretty nice. *Is that a need or a want?* I remembered the collection of silver dollars I'd saved when I was a paper boy and thought, *Hmm, maybe God has supplied all my needs, and I'm still asking Him for something extra.* So Theresa and I loaded up the TV, the stereo, my silver dollars, and some of her jewelry and went to a pawn shop. We got about $450 for all of it and were just able to pay for our food and rent that month.

I learned a very important lesson from that experience. God has often supplied our needs, but we expect Him to define His provision by a certain standard of living we've set for ourselves. We tell Him we can't afford to do what He's asking us to do because we have to make a payment on that late model car we stretched our budget to get or we can't make our house payment on the nice home we thought we deserved. Don't get me wrong—God isn't opposed to our having and enjoying some of these things over and above our basic needs. But He doesn't want us to define those luxuries as our needs and demand that He meet them. We have to keep needs and wants in perspective.

We have to keep needs and wants in perspective.

That distinction aside, Paul gives us three very specific conditions about the promise of verse 19. If you're serious about God's peace and contentment, you need to take His promises seriously and know who they're for and how to apply them.

Condition 1: This is not for unbelievers. Paul is not making a blanket promise to everyone out there that God will always meet all their needs. He is writing to a church, and the provision of God is given to those who are "in Christ Jesus." God loves everyone, but He does not commit Himself to meet the needs of those who resist Him and remain outside of Christ.

Condition 2: This is not for all believers. I don't think every Christian can claim this promise. I don't believe it applies to believers who are living in willful disobedience or who are not honoring God in their finances. Christians can be disobedient in major areas of our lives. We can be completely reckless and self-centered with our finances, and I don't believe God is assuring us that He will always meet our needs under those conditions. He is gracious, and we have all experienced wonderful provision at times when we were not necessarily walking closely with Him. His provision is not dependent on our being perfect. But is His provision guaranteed whether we are following Him obediently or not? I don't think so. Paul had already commended the Philippians for their faithful attitude and actions and sacrificially meeting his needs, and this promise is given in that context. This promise is true for those in Christ who are seeking first God's kingdom and His righteousness (Matthew 6:33) in the arena of their finances.

Condition 3: This is for believers who choose to walk by faith. And in the context of this passage of Philippians, the evidence of faith is sacrificial giving. This promise is for when God's children say, "Lord, I want to obey You. From my love for You and the compassion in my heart, I want to give of my time, talent, and money to honor You with the first portion of my income or meet this specific need. And if You don't catch me, I'm in a bind." This particular promise is God's way of saying, "I'll catch you. I'm there." He is reassuring those who live generously and sacrificially that they are not going to lose out in the process.

The way to unlock God's promises is by faith—trusting in Him even when everything's on the line. More than anything, God wants to deepen and develop our relationship with Him. Being a follower of Jesus is not fundamentally about outward moral behavior, engaging in the right activities, serving in the church, giving a certain amount of money, or anything else that could be translated into a formula. He is after sons and daughters who love Him and express their love by trusting Him enough to do what He says because they know He is good and always has their best in mind.

God longs for His children to take steps of faith so He can bless them.

Hebrews 11:6 says that it's impossible to please God without faith—that those who come to Him must (1) believe that He really, truly exists and (2) know that He rewards those who diligently seek Him. Don't miss the significance of that. While many people see Him as a punisher of those who don't seek Him, He is actually eager to reward those who do. God longs for His children to take steps of faith so He can bless them. In the context of faith, He promises to take care of us.

To bring this back to our financial needs and this specific promise in Philippians, debt and financial messes are often evidence that we have a need for immediate gratification and are looking for peace and contentment in things that money can buy. We've seen how that's a dead end. God's response is to say that if we learn to release our future to Him, trust Him, walk with Him, and align with His nature and character, He'll satisfy all our needs. He even goes above and beyond that and satisfies many of our wants too; He richly provides all things for us to enjoy (1 Timothy 6:17). But this promise guarantees that our basic needs of food, clothing, and shelter will always be covered.

The Law of the Harvest

There's a principle behind this promise, and it goes all the way back to the Old Testament. It's found throughout Scripture, from Genesis to Revelation, originating in the character of God and evident in the life of Jesus. It's foundational to the kingdom of God. It's called the Law of the Harvest.

There are other names for it: the law of sowing and reaping, or the law of reciprocity. But however you position it, it is the way the kingdom of God works. In a passage that was not specifically about finances but certainly applies to them, Jesus shared this kingdom principle with His followers: "Give, and it will be given to you. A good measure, pressed down, shaken together and running over, will be poured into your lap. For with the measure you use, it will be measured to you" (Luke 6:38). In other words, whether you use a fifty-five-gallon drum or a teaspoon, you'll find things coming back to you in the same measure you give them.

The world says to get, get, and get some more, to go out and acquire as much as you can so you can be comfortable, significant, strong, and secure. God says the opposite—to give, give, and give some more because you are already significant and secure in Christ, and your demonstration of trust in Him will be rewarded accordingly. Where the world tries to judge, protect, look out for self-interests, and accumulate things, you are free to love, forgive, have compassion, and give. When you live in that freedom, God blesses you with ample return on everything you've given. Whatever you pour out, He fills back up in abundance.

> You'll find things coming back to you in the same measure you give them.

This is not just a spiritual secret. It's evident even in nature. "Unless a kernel of wheat falls to the ground and dies, it remains only a single seed. But if it dies, it produces many seeds" (John 12:24). Creation declares the glory of God. This is how He has made the world. You can take grains of wheat and put them in the ground, and whatever you planted will multiply. You could have ground up that grain to make more bread, but by taking a portion of your harvest and planting it again, you get a greater harvest.

But here's the tricky part, the primary reason so many people neglect this profound principle: You rarely reap in the same season you sow. Seed takes time to grow. Many people don't see the fruit of their investments right away and give up. They decide it's better to get what they can while they can get it. The Law of the Harvest delays gratification but brings in much more fruit in the end. "A good measure, pressed down, shaken together and running over, will be poured into your lap."

Jesus applied the Law of the Harvest to His own life. He became like that grain of wheat that died in the ground but produced a great harvest.

> Being found in appearance as a man,
>   he humbled himself
>   by becoming obedient to death—
>   even death on a cross!
>
> Therefore God exalted him to the highest place
>   and gave him the name that is above every name,
> that at the name of Jesus every knee should bow,
>   in heaven and on earth and under the earth,
> and every tongue acknowledge that Jesus Christ is
>   Lord,
>   to the glory of God the Father. (Philippians
>   2:8–10)

With His very life, Jesus demonstrated that the way to receive is to give. He proved the ultimate secret of contentment.

Jesus applied the same secret of life, peace, and contentment to us. "Whoever wants to save their life will lose it, but whoever loses their life for me will save it" (Luke 9:24). Many people look at a verse like that with dread because they recognize that, at least on the surface, denying yourself and taking up an instrument of death seems literally to be a dead end.

This is where cognitive dissonance begins to do its work in us, isn't it? What seems at first to be dreadful is actually the key to life. We see it in nature; farmers use it all the time. We see it in Jesus; it's the means of our salvation. We see it throughout Scripture; it shows up again and again in the lives of biblical characters and the teachings of prophets and apostles. And if it's true—if this is an axiomatic, foundational truth of the kingdom of God—we must begin thinking completely differently about the way we live.

Seeing life in a different way is, of course, only a first step. It's a crucial one—we live in new ways only when we see in new ways—but we actually have to walk this out. And it's an exciting but sometimes scary process. If you're tired of hearing those stories of supernatural, timely provision in other people's lives and think they happen only with missionaries, pastors, and famous people, you need to know that this is possible for anybody who chooses to walk by genuine faith.

Be patient and persistent. You can experience miraculous stories too.

Step out, live, give, and care for others. Put the needs of others ahead of your wants. Then be patient and persistent. You can experience miraculous stories too.

That's because God is a rewarder of those who trust Him. Steps of faith may be counterintuitive, like giving generously in a time of financial strain, but He loves that kind of faith. There have been times when I really wrestled with the question of whether I trusted Him to take care of me; sometimes my answer was "maybe." You don't always feel like taking steps of faith, so don't make the mistake of overspiritualizing this process. Just obey. And expect God to provide.

Be careful, though. Many prosperity teachers have taken this kingdom principle and perverted it. They have persuaded vulnerable Christians to give them money in order to get money from God. We never "give to get." We give in accordance with God's will to honor Him, express our love, and meet the spiritual, emotional, and physical needs of others.

Applying the Law of the Harvest in Real Life

Paul takes us through that process in his second letter to the church at Corinth. The context of chapters 8–9 is a collection Paul is taking up for fellow believers in need. He refers to the generosity of the Macedonian churches as an example and says he has also been boasting to the Macedonians about the Corinthians' generosity. Threaded throughout this passage is the Law of the Harvest, the principle of sowing and reaping that is so deeply embedded in Scripture. In his words to the Corinthians, Paul outlines several important steps in how this process of living by faith works for ordinary people like you and me.

● *The Principle Restated:*

When you have a need, plant a seed.

Jesus broadly applied this agricultural picture to love, grace, and forgiveness in Luke 6:38. Paul applies the same principle specifically to the use of our resources. "Remember this: Whoever sows sparingly will also reap sparingly, and whoever sows generously will also reap generously" (2 Corinthians 9:6). If a farmer plants a few grains of wheat, he'll grow a little bit of wheat. If he plants thousands of seeds, he'll grow a lot. That's what Paul is saying here. It's very simple. If you want a lot, plant a lot. If you have a need, plant a seed.

This absolutely applies to financial situations, but please understand that it's much bigger than that. You'll see this work in virtually every area of life. What do we tell people who complain about not having any friends? We tell them to "be a friend" to someone else. The world says to get friends, to build yourself up, and focus on your own fulfillment through relationships. What would happen if we turned that around and focused our energy on offering friendship to others? What if we made it a priority to meet other people's needs and longings in relationships? Do you think that would end up being less fulfilling for us? No, when we sow generously, we reap generously.

The same is true with time. I can't figure out how this works, but when I have an overwhelming to-do list and not enough time to fit it in, I'm usually reminded of my long-ago commitment to give God the first part of each day. So I set my alarm a half hour earlier and give Him more time. What happens? He multiplies the fruit of the other hours in the day.

It's amazing how this works. If you need more time, give some time away. If you need love and affection, give love and affection. If you need friends, be a friend. If you need more grace for your mistakes, be more gracious toward those around you. Warning: Don't walk away if nothing happens immediately. Remember, we hardly ever reap in the same season we sow. I am completely confident you'll see some dramatic changes over time. More importantly, that's what Scripture promises. This is how God works.

I came across a parable years ago that helps me picture and remember this amazing kingdom principle:

> Once there was a man lost in the desert, near death from thirst. He wandered almost aimlessly through the burning sand for many days, growing weaker by the moment. At long last, he saw an oasis in the distance, palm trees indicating that there was water. He stumbled forward feverishly, fell beneath the shade of the trees, that he finally might quench his tortured thirst.
>
> But then he noticed something strange about this oasis: Instead of a pool of water or a spring bubbling up from the ground, he found a pump. And beside the pump were two objects: a small jar of water and a parchment note. The note explained that the leather gasket within the pump must be saturated with water for the pump to work. Within the jar was just enough water for this purpose. The note also warned that the reader should not drink from the jar. Every single drop must be poured into the opening at the base of the pump to soak the heat-dried gasket. Then, as the leather softens and expands, an unlimited supply of sweet water would be available. The parchment's final instructions were to refill the jar for the next traveler.
>
> The man faced a dilemma. He was dying of thirst, and he had found water. Not much, of course, and likely not

enough even to save his life. But it seemed the height of folly to pour it away down the base of the pump. On the other hand, if the note was accurate, by pouring out the small quantity of water, he would then have all the water he wanted. What should he do?[1]

What would you do? It's a simple choice, really. If the note isn't true, you will probably die anyway. But if the note is true, you'd be a fool not to follow its instructions. It would be the smartest, wisest, most important thing you could do. Yet pouring out that water seems insane, doesn't it?

The majority of people in the world are consuming whatever is available to them. Those who trust God and understand the Law of the Harvest are wiser than that. By faith, we pour out what we have in order to get an unlimited supply of it— good measure, pressed down, shaken together, running over.

That's the promise of Philippians 4:19. It actually creates a dilemma for us because we have to decide if we are going to believe it and take steps of faith or ignore and reject it as unlikely or untrue. Deciding it's true may take you down a path you've never been on before, and that's always a little scary, but it leads to powerful experiences with God and those stories of supernatural provision that we all love to hear. I believe you'll find that the promise really does apply to you.

● The Procedure Outlined:

Give with the right motive.

There's a temptation in this promise, isn't there? Many people will turn it around for self-centered purposes and think, *Ah, so if I want to get rich, all I need to do is plant some seeds.* And they are following the letter of the Law of the Harvest but not the spirit behind it.

Rest assured: I am not teaching a health-and-wealth gospel here. We don't give in order to get. But in God's economy, giving does have certain consequences. Receiving is a by-product of giving because God is generous and wants to bless those who trust Him. He is not telling us to work a system; He is asking us to trust and become like Him—a generous giver who gives from compassion and love. Someone following a "me-centered" health-and-wealth gospel misses that part of the equation. Scripture strongly warns those among us who teach this (1 Timothy 6:3–11).

God's promises do not give us any license to try to cut a deal with Him. The Law of the Harvest is not a mathematical formula. When you hear someone say that if you give God a hundred, He'll give you a thousand, that person is playing a game. That makes God like a vending machine, and it disqualifies us from the promise.

> **The Law of the Harvest is not a mathematical formula.**

Paul says it's important to give with the right motive. If you're giving to get, it's not giving. "Each of you should give what you have decided in your heart to give, not reluctantly or under compulsion, for God loves a cheerful giver" (2 Corinthians 9:7). Notice the phrasing: "what you have decided"; "not reluctantly"; not "under compulsion"; "a cheerful giver." That is full of right motives. You don't give that way when someone else is twisting your arm and making false promises. You give that way when your heart overflows with the goodness of God.

Giving "what you have decided" means being thoughtful about it. Thoughtful giving comes from pure motives. It isn't manipulative. I remember going to church when I was young and, if I was in a good mood, giving five bucks or so. If I wasn't in a good mood, maybe a dollar. And if I was on top of the world, I might throw in a twenty and be amazed at how generous I was. I didn't know anything about the Bible. It was kind of like going to a movie and paying for a ticket only if the movie was good. My giving was emotionally rooted in the moment.

God says not to give that way. Your motives need to be thoughtful. As we saw in Paul's other letter to the Corinthians, he recommended bringing your offering on the first day of the week according to the ways God has blessed you that week (1 Corinthians 16:1–2). It requires taking mental inventory of His goodness toward you. That's a good motive.

You also need to give "not reluctantly" and "not under compulsion." That means giving enthusiastically, not merely as an obligation or out of peer pressure. It's voluntary. You aren't responding to someone who ranted and raved about how delinquent everyone is in their donations, or to someone who is manipulating emotions and twisting arms. Anytime I hear a manipulative message about giving, I take that as a sign from God not to give there. I don't want to give under compulsion. I do want to give, but not with the wrong motive. I need to find a place where I can do that and trust that those who are asking me to give are full of integrity and inviting me to follow God's directions and not their agenda.

That leads to the final phrase: "God loves a cheerful giver." The word used here for *cheerful* is the same word we get *hilarious* from. We give with that kind of lighthearted joy. We get the word *miserable* from *miser* because stingy people, the Scrooges of the world, are generally not very happy. That tight-fisted spirit is right in line with the world's agenda of acquiring and accumulating, but it never leads to peace or contentment. Have you ever known anybody whose credit cards are maxed out and whose debts are piled up to be at peace? Neither have I. The Law of the Harvest says to give, release, trust, love, and be generous with your grace, forgiveness, time, talents, energies, money, and resources, and to do it from your heart. Be tenderhearted and compassionate. Give "hilariously." Be happy about it. And God's goodness will come running over, back into your lap. This is not a health-and-wealth gospel. It's a give-and-enjoy gospel. There's a world of difference.

This is not a health-and-wealth gospel. It's a give-and-enjoy gospel.

Still not convinced? Stay with me as God invites you to *know for certain* that when you exercise the Law of the Harvest, He's more than got you covered.

● *The Promise Expanded:*

God will give you everything you need in every area of your life.

Try a fun exercise. Count how many times the words *all* and *every* show up in these verses:

171

God is able to bless you abundantly, so that in *all* things at *all* times, having *all* that you need, you will abound in *every* good work. As it is written:

> "They have freely scattered their gifts to the poor;
>   their righteousness endures forever."

Now he who supplies seed to the sower and bread for food will also supply and increase your store of seed and will enlarge the harvest of your righteousness. You will be enriched in *every* way so that you can be generous on *every* occasion, and through us your generosity will result in thanksgiving to God. (2 Corinthians 9:8–11, italics added)

God is able to bless you abundantly in all things at all times, and you will be enriched in every way. Why? Not so you can hoard it and break the cycle of giving and receiving, but so you can be generous on every occasion and perpetuate the cycle. That's a sweeping promise.

Can God really mean this? A lot of people read these words and think, *That hasn't been my experience.* But if they think it through, they have to admit that this kind of giving hasn't been their experience either. Might I tactfully suggest that those things are connected?

Most Christians don't give of their time, talents, and re-sources this way. In fact, only 5 percent of Americans who claim the name of Christ even give a tithe of 10 percent of their income, let alone practice radical generosity.[2] Why? Either because they have never been taught, or they don't believe, or perhaps because it's frightening. What if God doesn't come through? That's why Paul spells out the promise: God is able. And His blessing comes to us at *all* times in *every* way.

Does this apply to financial needs? Emotional needs? Relational issues? Career paths? Well, what does "all" mean to you? It's comprehensive. Again, this doesn't mean God will satisfy every want in all these areas. It does mean, however, that He is watching over your needs and concerns, abundantly willing and able—and, in fact, eager—to meet you there.

Just as the Law of the Harvest suggests, Paul is giving us an agricultural metaphor throughout this passage. But look what he does in verse 9: "Now he who supplies *seed* to the sower and *bread* for food will also supply and increase your *store of seed* and will *enlarge the harvest of your righteousness*" (emphasis added). Do you see that? He suddenly unveils it as a spiritual issue.

God gives us seed to begin with, our provision to invest. It's different for everybody, but for everybody it's something. He also gives us bread for food. That's today's sustenance—His provision for our immediate needs. But He also supplies and increases our store of seed—the portion a farmer uses to put back into the ground, the remainder we can use to invest. Why? To "enlarge the harvest of our righteousness" so that we "will be enriched in every way." The reason God gives us increase is so our harvest will increase spiritually, emotionally, relationally, financially, and "every" other way. And the reason He expands our harvest in all these ways is not so we can have more, do more, and be more, but *so we can be even more generous*, starting the cycle all over again—all for the ultimate purpose of helping, caring for, and loving others in a way that causes them to look up and give thanks to God.

I like the way Randy Alcorn puts it: "God prospers me not to raise my standard of living, but to raise my standard of giving."[3] But it doesn't just happen. We have to take a step of faith to participate in the process of giving, receiving, increase of seed, increase of harvest, greater generosity, thanksgiving to God.

We have to take a step of faith to participate in the process.

One of the things Theresa and I have done is to draw a financial income line for what we need to live on. As long as I live, however much God gives me over that line, that's what I'm going to give away. I think that's something everyone should consider doing. You may strategically raise or lower that line at different seasons of life, but it is helpful in keeping your finances oriented around sacrifice and generosity. Otherwise, compromise creeps in. As we receive increase, we tend to habitually increase our standard of living but not our percentage of giving. Sadly, many sincere Christians have given 10 percent of their income for twenty or thirty years while their income has doubled or tripled. They give almost the way they pay bills—and miss the joy and adventure of the supernatural movement of God's Spirit in their finances.

Paul was encouraging this church to give more, not because it was easy for them but because it was part of God's purpose in blessing others and blessing them through their own gift. Paul was going to take this collection to Jerusalem, where

Jewish believers were going through hard times from a famine. Those brothers and sisters would eat the food that was provided through that collection and give thanks to God, praising Him for His provision. But they would know He doesn't usually provide in a vacuum. He provides through His people.

That's our calling—to be vessels of provision. We see a need, God puts it on our heart to do something about it, and the people who are blessed by that provision thank Him for it. Then He provides for us because we let Him provide for others through us.

The world's mentality is to see resources as part of one big, limited pie. They're limited. You have to get your piece of the pie because if you don't, there won't be enough left for you. That's not how it works in the kingdom of God because King Jesus has unlimited resources. He's the pie maker. When He finds people who will give away not only their slice but whole pies, He'll provide a truckload. He loves faith, and He rewards those who diligently seek Him.

He gives us an abundance so we can be abundantly generous.

Over the years, I've met godly men and women who have taken God up on His promise to be radically generous. They all tell me the same thing: "You can't out-give God." As one elderly saint told me, some people are streams, and some people are reservoirs. The water runs through streams, but it stays in reservoirs. When God finds a man or woman who will be a stream, He keeps pouring out the blessing because He knows it doesn't get stuck. It passes on to those who need it. He gives us an abundance so we can be abundantly generous.

An Invitation to Test Him

I remember as a kid playing with some friends on a roof. I don't know if we were allowed up there, but there we were. And the roof of the neighboring house looked pretty close— close enough to make you want to run fast and see if you could jump from one to the other. We knew it was risky. That's what made it so tempting. But it was dangerous enough for us to know it was a bad idea.

That is, until someone said, "I dare you!" That one phrase turns something that looks like a bad idea into a test of your manhood. It's hard to resist when you're twelve years old. And when it's followed by "I *double* dare you," well . . . it was almost an obligation. I landed on the edge, right on my stomach, and slid down. The roof was fine. I was okay. My ego was bruised.

When God says, "I dare you," it's a different story. He isn't provoking our egos. He's testing our faith, and the only reason He would do that is with our good in mind. I know of only one place in Scripture where He does that, and it's related to this issue of having a generous spirit, taking steps of faith, and releasing what we have so the Law of the Harvest can have its result. He so wants us to experience the reality of His supernatural power and grace that He gives us a very tangible, specific way to put our faith on the line and depend on Him.

The prophet Malachi was speaking to exiles who had returned to Jerusalem and were reestablishing Judah's culture and worship. It had been a long process, and some of them had grown lax in their commitments. One of those commitments was God's instructions to tithe—to give Him 10 percent of their income or harvest. So God dared them to see what would happen if they were faithful in this area. "Bring the whole tithe into the storehouse, that there may be food in my house. Test me in this . . . and see if I will not throw open the floodgates of heaven and pour out so much blessing that there will not be room enough to store it" (Malachi 3:10). He put His own reputation on the line. He just wanted them to take a step of faith.

Old Testament instructions for giving amounted to about 23 percent of a family's income to support the worship, social needs, and government of Israel's theocracy. Here God emphasizes the basic 10-percent tithe. Jesus urged people to keep tithing but to realize that the main point of the Law was justice and compassion, not a monetary amount. The number really isn't the key issue, but it's a great starting point. And I've seen God do amazing things in the lives of people who commit to it.

I'll never forget teaching this passage and principle when I pastored in Santa Cruz, California. The church was almost all new believers, and I was prompted to challenge everyone to "test God" for ninety days to give Him the first 10 percent of their income, live on the remaining 90 percent, and see what happens. The church was doing fine financially, so it wasn't about any need. I even told them that if they were concerned about any hidden agenda to give it to a charity that feeds orphans and the poor rather than to a church.

I could tell story after story of how people tested God in this promise and found Him faithful. A Chinese girl who came to faith brought her first portion the week she became a Christian. She shared with me how she had twice as many customers the next week. A man who was pretty well off but decided to increase his giving from 10 to 20 percent became the top salesman in a major company. A family realized after the ninety-day challenge that they had never had such peace in their home in all the years they had been married. Another family was forced to develop a budget, and that discipline carried over into multiple areas of their family life. I have a thick file folder of stories from people writing to tell how they had "tested God" and He rewarded their faith. Again and again, God keeps His promises.

I'm not saying you will necessarily be financially blessed if you tithe. I do believe God will take care of your needs, but this is not a formula for success. The promise is that if you give, God will give back in areas your heart needs the most. If you take steps of faith in any area of life and put God's promises to the test, He will show Himself to be faithful. You will be blessed in the areas your heavenly Father knows will mean the most to you. Into your need, He will bring contentment. Into your emptiness, He will bring fulfillment. And into the trials and turbulence of your life, He will bring peace.

QUESTIONS FOR DISCUSSION AND REFLECTION

1. What is the relationship between experiencing personal peace and living by faith?

2. Why is giving such an integral part of activating the faith in our lives that leads to peace?

3. In what area of your life do you have a great need? What would planting a seed look like in this area?

4. What specific step of faith or obedience has God directed you to take?

CONCLUSION

We started out with peace. We ended with provision. Why? Because our uncertainty about the future, our concern for our own well-being, and our desire to be fully provided for and have all our needs met are very often at the root of our lack of peace. But, as you know, there are literally hundreds, even thousands of potential events, situations, relationships, trends, messages, and moods that can unsettle us. We each have certain triggers and temptations in our lives that will disrupt our peace if we let them. The dominant message of this book is this: Don't let them.

In order to understand how to live out that message, we've looked at a lot of truths from chapter 4 of Philippians and other passages in this book, all of them aimed at bringing us into God's *shalom*: the peace, wholeness, fullness, and completeness of His will for us. In that place of peace, we resolve conflicts with others, get free from our anxieties, find contentment in difficult circumstances, develop compassion and generosity, and overcome the temptations of greed. But none of that happens without intentional, specific steps of faith. Simply agreeing with God's principles isn't the key to experiencing their benefits. We have to apply them. We have to make moment-by-moment choices, in even the most trying and chaotic situations, to walk in the peace we have already been given. And that means making decisions that might feel risky. In many ways, a step of faith takes us on a journey into the unknown.

But even though we don't always know where faith will lead us, we do know the character of the Faithful One. The promises He gives us are not speculations or wishful thinking. They do come with certain conditions, but they are not lined with fine print that only the superspiritual can see. The principles of His Word are not relevant only for culturally different people in an ancient world. They are for us today, and they are life changing. I invite you to commit to them—to take God at His word, test Him in His promises, and experience how He brings His *shalom*—His supernatural peace and wholeness—into your heart and life.

Remember, you already have the peace Jesus gave you. It's the same peace that sustained Him through numerous conflicts and disputes about His work and His messages, much opposition, many trials and temptations, and the ultimate sacrifice on behalf of a fallen, chaotic world. The Prince of Peace laid down His life so we might be able to walk in the peace He brings. It's a priceless gift. Face every crisis, every difficulty, every challenge of life with a profound, life-changing statement that gratefully receives, embraces, and enjoys that gift: *I choose peace.*

I Choose Peace
Teaching Series Notes

Dear Fellow Pastors, Small Group Leaders, Sunday School Teachers, and Entrepreneurs,

I hope this book has been a help to you, and if it has, I know many of you will want to teach, revise, and communicate this message of peace to others.

The foundation for this book came from my *I Choose Peace* teaching series, which we've made available to help you share this truth.

What follows are message notes to accompany parts 1 through 4 of the series. I encourage you to listen to the series for additional insights. Go to **www.LivingontheEdge .org/I-Choose-Peace-Book** to find these messages, which you can play directly from the site or download as audio MP3 files. To round out the teaching, parts 5 and 6 of the series are also available online.

The discussion questions in these notes are the same as those found in the preceding chapters. I encourage you to use the notes as well as the discussion questions when you teach these messages to help your listeners or group members apply these truths to their daily lives, just as readers of this book have done.

Message notes to all my other teachings are available to download for free on the Chip Ingram App or at Livingon theEdge.org. My heart's desire is to help you communicate God's Word in a way that is biblical, practical, clear, and life changing. It's an honor to partner with you.

Partnering Together to Share God's Peace,

CEO and Teaching Pastor, Living on the Edge

PART 1

IN RELATIONAL CONFLICT

Philippians 4:1-5

Introduction: Three Approaches to Peace

- Inward
- Outward
- Upward

The World's Peace

The absence of disturbance and hostility, free from internal and external strife.

God's Peace: *Shalom*

1. Complete soundness or wholeness of health
2. Harmony in relationships
3. Success and fulfillment of purpose
4. Victory over one's enemies

Peace I leave with you; my peace I give you. I do not give to you as the world gives. Do not let your hearts be troubled and do not be afraid.

Jesus of Nazareth, John 14:27

With what one person would you most like to be at peace?

Choosing Peace in Relational Conflict (Philippians 4:1-5)

The context

Therefore, my brothers and sisters, you whom I love and long for, my joy and crown, stand firm in the Lord in this way, dear friends! (v. 1)

The plea for unity

I plead with Euodia and I plead with Syntyche to be of the same mind in the Lord. (v. 2)

The request for competent counsel

Yes, and I ask you, my true yokefellow, to help these women who have [contended] with me for the gospel, along with Clement and the rest of my fellow workers, whose names are in the Book of Life. (v. 3 BSB)

The command concerning relational focus

Rejoice in the Lord always. I will say it again: Rejoice! (v. 4)

The command concerning personal responsibility

Let your gentleness be evident to all. The Lord is near. (v. 5)

5 Ways to Diffuse Relational Conflict

1. Resolve to stop PROCRASTINATING. (v. 1)
2. Reevaluate your EXPECTATIONS. (v. 2)
3. Get competent outside HELP. (v. 3)
4. Refuse to allow ONE relationship to ruin your life. (v. 4)
5. Remember a right RESPONSE is more important than being RIGHT. (v. 5)

Discussion Questions

1. On a scale of 1–10, rank the level of stress and concern you are currently experiencing from any problem relationship.

2. Why does relational conflict rob us of peace? What price are you paying to allow this to continue?

3. What specific steps does the apostle Paul give to help resolve relational conflict? List them and discuss each.

4. Is there a relationship in your life that calls for you to follow this pattern? When and how will you follow God's plan for peace (as far as it depends on you)?

5. Who could help you turn your good intention into action this week?

PART 2:
IN ANXIOUS MOMENTS

Philippians 4:6-7

Introduction

Jesus's promise

These things I have spoken to you, so that in Me you may have peace. In the world you have tribulation, but take courage; I have overcome the world.

John 16:33 NASB

- What exactly is anxiety?
- What causes anxiety?
  - Fear of the future
  - Conflict in the present
  - Regrets over the past
- How does anxiety affect us?

How can we overcome anxiety?

Choosing God's Peace When Anxiety Strikes (Philippians 4:6-7)

Do not be anxious about anything, but in every situation, by prayer and petition, with thanksgiving, present your requests to God. And the peace of God, which transcends all understanding, will guard your hearts and your minds in Christ Jesus.

Philippians 4:6–7

<u>Nothing</u> be anxious about
But in everything
- by prayer
- by petition
- with thanksgiving
- the <u>requests</u> of you <u>let be made known</u> to God.

And the <u>peace</u> of God
↓
   (surpassing all <u>understanding</u>)
     will <u>guard</u> the <u>hearts</u> of you
     and
     the thoughts of you
       in Christ Jesus

The Commands = the What

1. Negatively =
2. Positively =

Four Key Words = the How

PRAYER = worship and adoration.

PETITION = focus on your needs.

THANKSGIVING = focus on what God has done.

REQUESTS = outline your specific requests.

The Promise = the Why

1. Peace and anxiety cannot COEXIST.
2. Anxiety and biblical prayer cannot COEXIST.

Summary

Biblical PRAYER is God's antidote to anxiety.

This week, every time you feel anxious, remember the following word picture . . .

When ANXIETY pounds at the door of your heart, let PRAYER answer it as you RUN into your Father's arms!

Discussion Questions

1. When do you tend to be anxious?

2. What are the issues in your life that are "strangling" and "stressing" you mentally and emotionally?

3. How will you put this message into practice? Who will help/encourage you in your battle to overcome anxiety?

4. Is there a relationship in your life that calls for you to follow this pattern? Who in your relationship network struggles with anxiety and needs your help?

PART 3:
IN A BROKEN WORLD

Philippians 4:8–9

Introduction: Are You Feeding or Starving Your Fear?

University of Tennessee – 12-year study

Psychologically: "We are what we eat"

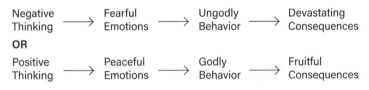

OR

Summary

Science and Scripture agree:

1. We are a product of our THOUGHT life. (Proverbs 23:7)
2. Our EMOTIONS flow from our thought life. (Romans 8:6)
3. What we allow to enter our mind is the most important DECISION we make each and every day. (Romans 12:2)

The Question: How can we choose peace in a broken world?

The Answer:

Finally, brethren, whatever is true, whatever is honorable, whatever is right, whatever is pure, whatever is lovely, whatever is of good repute, if there is any excellence and if anything worthy of praise, dwell on these things. The things you have learned and received and heard and seen in me, practice these things, and the God of peace will be with you.

Philippians 4:8–9 NASB 1995

Command #1: DWELL on these things . . .   Philippians 4:8

True: Objectively true, that which conforms to reality vs. things that are deceptive, illusions that promise peace and happiness.

Pre-view question: Is this TRUE or FALSE?

Honorable: "Sober," "serious," "worthy of respect," "inspires awe"—it refers to those things which reflect the weighty purposes of a believer's life.

Pre-view question: Does this HONOR or DISHONOR?

Right: "Righteous"; used in New Testament to refer to the Father, Jesus, God's actions, God's character. It pictures doing what is right when tempted.

Pre-view question: Is this morally RIGHT or WRONG?

Pure: From the same root word as "holy." It means free from defilement; sexual and moral purity in thought, word, and deed.

Pre-view question: Will this CLEANSE or DIRTY my soul?

Lovely: "Attractive," "winsome," "beautiful"; it pictures those things that call forth a response of love and warmth within us vs. bitterness, criticism, and vengeance.

Pre-view question: Will this RENEW or HARDEN my heart?

Good Repute: That which is "commendable," "gracious," "admirable"; it literally means "fair speaking." It describes the things which are fit for God to hear vs. ugly words, false words, and impure words.

Pre-view question: Could I RECOMMEND this to someone who looks up to me?

Summary

Virtue and/or Praise: A summary of sorts to "think on" anything that has moral excellence and will inspire and motivate us to love God and others.

Command #2: Habitually PRACTICE these things... Philippians 4:9a

- Learned . . . Received: Appetite and application
- Heard . . . Saw: Instruction and modeling

Why? Your thought life determines your FUTURE. (Romans 8:5–8)

How? The principle of mind RENEWAL. (Romans 12:2)

Promise: The God of peace (*shalom*) will be WITH YOU. (Philippians 4:9b)

21 Minutes That Will Change Your Life

1. **Read:** The Bible	10 minutes
2. **Pray:** Talk with God	7 minutes
3. **Listen:** Sit quietly and listen	3 minutes
4. **Apply:** One specific truth, e.g., serve someone	1 minute

Discussion Questions

1. How does our thought life affect our emotions?

2. How would you describe the <u>quality</u> of your thought life? What adjustments do you sense God would have you make in what you **view, read,** and **think**?

3. Why is **habitual practice** of the truth so vital if we are to experience <u>God's peace</u>? Why does "duplicity" create <u>stress</u> and lack of peace in our lives?

4. What <u>insight</u> has God given you today to help you experience His **peace** in your life? How will you choose to cooperate with God's process in your life? Who will help you?

Resources

Reclaiming the Lost Art of Biblical Meditation by Robert Morgan

Good to Great in God's Eyes by Chip Ingram (Chapter 1: "Think Great Thoughts")

Topical Memory System by The Navigators Press

PART 4:
IN DIFFICULT CIRCUMSTANCES

Philippians 4:10–13

Introduction: What Would It Take for You to Be Content?

Definition

content happy enough with what one has or is; not desiring something more or different; satisfied.

Webster's Dictionary

The Problem: The horizon is always moving.

Two Historical Solutions

1. Conquer, achieve, and acquire until satisfied.
2. Desire less and less until it doesn't matter.

The Question: How can we be satisfied . . . today?

The Answer (Philippians 4:10–13)

The Occasion: A "Thank You" Note

I rejoiced greatly in the Lord that at last you have renewed your concern for me. Indeed, you have been concerned, but you had no opportunity to show it. (v. 10)

I am not saying this because I am in need, for I have
learned to be content whatever the circumstances. (v. 11)
I know what it is to be in need, and I know what it is to
have plenty. I have learned the secret of being content
in any and every situation, whether well fed or hungry,
whether living in plenty or in want. (v. 12)
I can do all this through him who gives me strength. (v. 13)

Conclusion

Contentment is not a thing to be achieved, but a secret to
be discovered.

Four Principles – Four Practices

- **Principle #1:** Our contentment is not dependent on
  our <u>circumstances</u>.
  - Practice = BE THANKFUL / GRATEFUL (v. 10)

- **Principle #2:** Contentment is an attitude we <u>learn</u> not
  a thing we achieve.
  - Practice = BE TEACHABLE (v. 11)

- **Principle #3:** Prosperity does not have the power to
  give us contentment; nor <u>poverty</u> the power to take it
  away.
  - Practice = BE FLEXIBLE / CHANGEABLE (v. 12)

- **Principle #4:** Only Christ has the power to give us a
  contentment that transcends all life's variables.
  - Practice = BE CONFIDENT / TRUSTING (v. 13)

Summary

Contentment is not passive acceptance of the status quo, but the positive assurance that God has supplied one's needs, and the consequent release from unnecessary desires.

Discussion Questions

1. Why is it so difficult to be genuinely content? What factors in our world make this so? What factors in our hearts make this so?

2. Why are both historical positions toward contentment doomed to failure?

3. Walk through each of the <u>principles</u> and <u>practices</u> and discuss how they relate to your present circumstances and attitudes about personal peace.

4. What <u>action step</u> will you take to reflect obedience to God's provision for your personal peace?

5. Take time to pray for one another in your group. Ask God to help each one to embrace His game plan for a life of personal peace.

NOTES

Chapter 1 Choose Peace in Relational Conflict

1. Matthew Arnold, *Literature and Dogma* (Boston: James R. Osgood, 1875), xv, 94, 207, 217, 231.

2. Kerry Patterson, Joseph Grenny, Ron McMillan, and Al Switzler, *Crucial Conversations: Tools for Talking When Stakes Are High* (New York: McGraw Hill, 2012).

Chapter 2 Choose Peace in Anxious Moments

1. Paul D. Meier, Frank B. Minirth, and Frank Wichern, *Introduction to Psychology and Counseling* (Grand Rapids: Baker, 1982).

Chapter 3 Choose Peace in a Broken World

1. Jack Haskins, "The Trouble with Bad News," Department of Communications, University of Tennessee, 1981.

2. Tommy Newberry, *The 4:8 Principle* (Carol Stream, IL: Tyndale, 2007).

3. Matt Maher, "Sing over Your Children," ThankYou Music, 2009.

Chapter 4 Choose Peace in Difficult Circumstances

1. T. R. Glover, *The Conflict of Religions in the Early Roman Empire* (London: Methuen, 1909), 67.

2. Todd A. Sinelli, *True Riches* (Santa Cruz, CA: Lit Torch Publishing, 2001).

3. Gary Smith, "Ali and His Entourage: Life after the End of the Greatest Show on Earth," *Sports Illustrated*, October 10, 2014, accessed March 2020, https://www.si.com/boxing/2014/10/10/muhammad-ali-entourage.

Chapter 5 Choose Peace in a Materialistic Culture

1. American Donor Trends, Barna Research Report, June 3, 2013.

Chapter 6 Choose Peace in Tests of Faith

1. Jim Carpenter, "The Parable of the Pump," *Discipleship*, no. 35, 1986, 15.

2. American Donor Trends.

3. Randy Alcorn, *The Treasure Principle* (Portland: Multnomah, 2001), 73.

REFERENCES

Barclay, William. *The Letters to the Philippians, Colossians, and Thessalonians.* The Daily Study Bible Series. Rev. ed. Philadelphia: Westminster, 1975.

———. *More New Testament Words.* New York: Harper & Row, 1958.

Gaebelein, Frank E. *Ephesians to Philemon.* The Expositor's Bible Commentary Series, vol. 11. Grand Rapids: Zondervan, 1980.

Hendriksen, William. *Philippians, Colossians and Philemon.* New Testament Commentary Series. Grand Rapids: Baker, 1979.

Martin, Ralph P. *Philippians.* Tyndale New Testament Commentaries. Grand Rapids: Eerdmans, 1989.

Meier, Paul D., Frank B. Minirth, and Frank Wichern. *Introduction to Psychology and Counseling.* Grand Rapids: Baker, 1982.

Meyer, F. B. *Devotional Commentary on Philippians.* Grand Rapids: Kregel, 1979.

Robertson, Archibald T. *The Epistles of Paul.* Word Pictures in the New Testament, vol. 4. Nashville: Broadman, 1931.

Sunukjian, Donald R. *Invitation to Philippians: Building a Great Church through Humility.* Wooster, OH: Weaver Book Company, 2014.

Turner, Nigel. *Christian Words: Concise Word Studies to Help Anyone Understand the Unique Vocabulary of the Greek New Testament.* Nashville: Thomas Nelson, 1982.

Wiersbe, Warren W. *The Bible Exposition Commentary: An Exposition of the New Testament Comprising the Entire "BE" Series.* Wheaton: Victor Books, 1989.

Wuest, Kenneth S., ed. *Philippians–Hebrews; The Pastoral Epistles–First Peter in the Last Days.* Wuest's Word Studies in the Greek New Testament, vol. 2. Grand Rapids: Eerdmans, 1986.

Chip Ingram is the founder and CEO of Living on the Edge, an international teaching and discipleship ministry. A pastor for over thirty-five years, Chip is the author of many books, including *Discover Your True Self*, *Marriage That Works*, *Culture Shock*, *The Real Heaven*, *The Real God*, *The Invisible War*, and *Love, Sex, and Lasting Relationships*. Chip and his wife, Theresa, have four grown children and twelve grandchildren and live in California.

See Yourself the Way
GOD SEES YOU

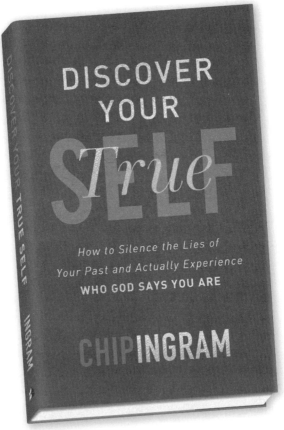

Chip Ingram wants to open your eyes to your true self, the "new you" that God sees; the person who is immeasurably valuable and beautiful. In this Scripture-soaked book, he shows you how getting God's perspective

- satisfies your search for significance
- undoes your shame
- makes you secure

- frees you from comparing yourself with others
- helps you discover your calling
- and more

BakerBooks
a division of Baker Publishing Group
www.BakerBooks.com

Available wherever books and ebooks are sold.

More from
CHIP INGRAM

Also Available from
CHIP INGRAM

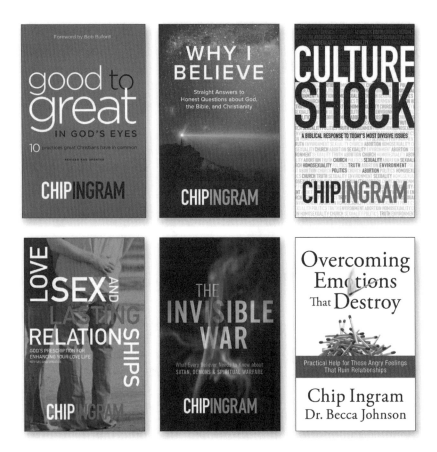

▰ LIVING ON THE EDGE™

Head to **LivingontheEdge.org** for Chip's
daily broadcast, free online courses,
digital downloads, group studies, and more!

DOWNLOAD THE CHIP INGRAM APP

The Chip Ingram App provides you with daily radio programs,
message notes, discipleship videos, Chip's blog, and more.
Download it now and listen when it's most convenient for you.

Find it on iTunes, Apple Play and CarPlay, or the Amazon Appstore

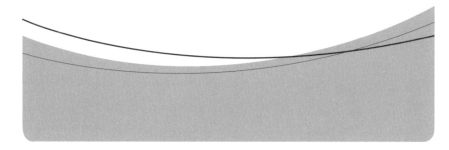